Sunny's S

By

Prameela Balasundaram

About the author

A postgraduate degree in English Literature from Bangalore University, a short study and work experience with persons with intellectual disability, with Lebenshilfe, the national parents group in Germany, and experiences of growing up with a niece with Downs Syndrome are some of the factors that have uniquely destined Prameela to found Samadhan, an NGO she set up in 1981 and also shaped Sunny's Story.

She has received both national and international recognition for her work in the form of awards from Inclusion International (the international network of people with intellectual disabilities and their families) and the World Bank.

Reviews

From North India, 'Sunny's story' is based on real events, starting with the disappearance of a young lad. Husband and wife wait late at night with mounting panic. She recalls 20 years ago, when she learnt that her baby has Downs Syndrome. What has become of Sunny, of the sunny temperament and trusting nature, in a world where the weak and simple may be brutally oppressed and abused? The story unfolds with reconstruction and imagination, from fragments that Sunny could tell later of his life with the 'platform people' at Jullundur, and Calcutta docks, mingled with family memories of incidents from his life with them. Somehow, on his haphazard travels, Sunny's simplicity had sent a signal to the kind of people who could respond in a gruffly protective way, despite common sense telling them to ignore him as just another among a million destitute wanderers. Sunny stood out as one who might be "a gift from the gods", sent to remind people to open themselves toward their unknown little brother. (M. Miles, researcher and practitioner in the field of disability in South Asia)

It tells the story of Sunny, a young man with Downs Syndrome, his adventures and the people who shared them with him and took care of him. Beautifully and sensitively written, with a depth of understanding for Sunny's condition and how it touched the lives of others – his family and friends. Poignantly highlighting the challenges faced by parents of children with intellectual disability, as well as the lack of awareness and limited support available in India. It could have ended very differently – the risks and dangers were huge. God was clearly protecting Sunny and putting people around him who would love him. (Jackie Nelson, friend and supporter)

Acknowledgement

To my sons Sanjay Edwin Balasundaram and Uday Mark Balasundaram, who with great understanding and love even as children, allowed me to invest my time and energy, which should have been theirs by right, into the building up of my NGO for other children, SAMADHAN.

Dedication

To my late husband, Rabindranath Balasundaram, for his empathy, unstinting financial support and for walking with me as long as God allowed him to do so.

EPISODE ONE: NEW DELHI

CHAPTER I

"He has not come back" said Kamal smiling, to still the panic which was slowly gathering in the pit of her stomach. The small bedroom in which she sat contained the bare minimum of furniture. A comfortable double bed with a small Kashmiri bedside table. A lamp with a bright red shade covered everything around it in a red glow. A dressing table under the window and an all purpose table which held an assortment of books. Mostly fiction. Sidney Sheldon prominent amongst them. These belonged to Kamal's husband and showed evidence of care and much usage.

The small clock that stood on the dressing table showed both hands at twelve. Midnight. Kamal walked towards the table and picked up the clock peering at it shortsightedly through the thick lenses of her spectacles, as if it was somehow giving her the wrong time. Could it really be so late? She looked out of the window and the light from the street lamp showed a stretch of the empty road. The bushes on the side of the road looked garish and artificial. She imagined her son, Sunny, walking down the road with his characteristic jaunty gait and the smile, which came so readily to him. So powerful was her visualization that for a moment she actually saw him. But of course there was no one on that road at this time of the night. Not even a lonely passerby. Who knew where Sunny went and what he did? For the millionth time she wished that she could understand what went on in his mind.

She turned back and walked over to the bed and slid under the warm *razai*. She picked up the book she was reading. It was one of those romances which she found amusing and which she forgot almost as soon as she had finished reading it. If someone had asked

1

her for details or names of the characters she would shake her head and smile vaguely. But it helped her to pass the time and at bedtime it was almost like taking a sedative, which sent her into quiet gentle sleep. She needed this now, more than any other night.

Her husband Prem sat watching the TV that perched precariously on the edge of the table along with an assortment of books, which were far too many for the small table. This second TV in their bedroom was a luxury, which they had both decided was not an indulgence but a necessity. When Kamal had retired from the travel agency where she had worked for the last twenty five years, she had been sent off with genuine regret and a handsome bonus in recognition of the many exhibitions she had designed and launched taking the richness of India to other countries and selling the package tours of her firm. One of the first things Kamal had done with the bonus was to purchase a small TV set for the exclusive use of Prem and herself. There was to be no more arguing about which channel to watch and who would watch what. Watching TV just before getting into bed had become a ritual. Though more often than not it was Prem who watched while Kamal looked over occasionally from the comfort of her bed.

Kamal knew that although Prem's eyes were glued to the screen he was not really registering anything. He made no response to her statement about Sunny. This was not very unusual. Prem was a man of few words and thirty-five years of married life made Kamal an expert in interpreting his silences. They were as eloquent as if he had spoken. Tonight however, Kamal needed something more. She sat up and the suddenness of her action made the *razai* fall to the ground. Prem looked up with concern and saw in her eyes what he had tried hard not to betray. It was panic. Pure, raw panic.

"He has been late before" he said gently, responding to her remark now. He spoke with a nonchalance he did not feel. "He will come home when he gets hungry. I hope you have some dinner ready for him." He laughed, hoping to get an answering smile from her and to show that she should not worry. But the white bleakness in her face wrenched at his heart. "The boy is a nuisance sometimes," he thought with unaccustomed irritation. He was mildly apprehensive but he honestly did not think there was serious cause for worry. Sunny will get a mouthful from me as soon as he comes in, he promised himself. But he wondered if it would do any good at all. Would Sunny even understand why he was being scolded?

Kamal realized that her husband was willing her to be quiet. His eyes said, "Be still. Everything will be alright if only we wait long enough. Everything will be alright." They had gone through this ritual before. At different times and with a different set of circumstances each time. She knew there was no use in pursuing the subject.

She quietly slid into bed and prepared herself for what she knew would be a long night, full of vague fears, until they heard Sunny come in. It was possible that he would come in making as much noise as an elephant, but it was always, always nerve wracking to have to wait for him on nights such as this.

Prem watched his wife take off her glasses, put her book aside, and close her eyes as if she was ready for sleep. The bedside lamp turned away from her face made her look soft and vulnerable. Looking at her lying there with eyes closed and her arms under her head, pretending that it was an evening like any other, brought Prem to the verge of an unaccustomed emotion. He wanted to get up and put his arms around her and reassure her that he was there for her. But he had never displayed such impulsive behavior ever, and years of restraint made it impossible for him to do so now. So he continued to sit where he was, while the TV screen flickered with brilliant color.

Kamal closed her eyes and gave herself up to the kaleidoscope of images that flashed through her head. Gradually it settled into a series of reminiscences. Sunny. One month old, chubby and beautiful. Sunny, smiling with eyes that crinkled delightfully. Sunny. His little snub nose. His little fingers. Stumpy but so cute. Only later,

3

much, much later, did all the physical signs she noted, but had not questioned, make sense to her. Like the stumpy fingers. The slanting eyes. The delightful little snub nose.

She thought back to the very first time that she had taken Sunny to Dr. Raut. She had gone over the events of that day so often that it now unrolled like a film montage in her mind's eye. With ease, Kamal now slipped into what she had done a hundred times before. Re-living Sunny's life and going over each event of his life however big or small with a patience born out of unconditional love.

CHAPTER II

It is twenty years ago. The year 1970. Kamal stands near the window in Dr. Raut's clinic, watching the gray drizzle soak the lawn and the white plastic garden chairs. The rain settling on the large prize roses is bending them over with their weight. The orange curtains hang heavy and listless and do little to cheer up the room. Two-year-old Sunny is fast asleep in her arms. Grayness. Everything is gray. The rain. The clinic. The way she feels. Drained and with a strange feeling of dread.

"So, what brings you out on such a miserable day?" Dr. Raut has come in behind her and his loud booming voice immediately reassures her. She turns to greet him and is genuinely happy to see him. A surge of hope brightens her face. Now that Dr. Raut is here, everything will be set right. Whatever it was that was wrong with Sunny will all be explained away now.

Dr. Raut is fit and ready to face the day and its quota of patients. A number of framed degrees and certificates proclaim his expertise in pediatrics and testify to his proficiency as doctor and as a man with the kind of skills to head many an organization. He has an extremely busy practice and he has agreed to see Kamal only because of his genuine fondness and regard for her. He had seen her safely through her first pregnancy and the sniffles and colds of her first son. He strides forward and takes her by the arm and leads her to a chair across from his table.

A large man with heavy shoulders, a large nose, and perpetually smelling of Old Spice, he is well known in the city of Delhi. Put a pipe in his mouth and a cravat round his neck and he will look at home in any British setting. Perhaps even passing off as one of the British gentry. With younger and newly qualified medical professionals opening their clinics on almost every street corner the kind of reputation he still enjoys says it all for him. He becomes all doctor now.

"So, it's only when your babies fall sick that you think of me," he says, attempting a joke. Kamal smiles on cue.

"What is wrong with this one?" continues Dr. Raut; "Your second son isn't it? Colic? Cold, or a touch of something..." He bends over the sleeping baby and all his years of training does not prevent the sudden stiffening of his body as he stops speaking in mid-sentence. Kamal can hear the clock tick loudly and noises from the waiting room next door. Her heart does a flip-flop and comes to rest again, thudding painfully.

Dr. Raut smiles at Kamal, but he is agonized. His mind races frantically. How many times had he been in such situations? It was always a nightmare. But this was Kamal. Old friend. And this child in her arms, unmistakably Downs Syndrome. There is unfortunately no possibility of an error. This chromosomal defect is easily recognizable and characterized by intellectual disability. This little baby will always be behind, always slow, and yes, face it, always a problem.

His mind flashes back briefly to a heated debate in the second year of his medical college. The subject being discussed was what a doctor should do when confronted with a child with an intellectual disability. There was no cure and the only answer was to train parents to look after these children themselves. But the million-dollar question, of course, was who would first tell the parents that their child was disabled?

Among swirls of gray cigarette smoke and mugs of pale coffee many had voted for euthanasia. Their reasoning was supported by a desire to spare the parents from a life of certain pain. Why go through life with a child who you know will create problems? Dr. Raut had never subscribed to the euthanasia view but had had no other solutions. After all these years, he realizes he still does not have an answer.

Dr. Raut dislikes intensely the responsibility his profession puts on him in such situations. Obviously Kamal does not suspect anything. Here she is looking at him as if he was some miracle worker. She does not have the slightest idea that her son is not normal and never will be. That he is in fact a child with an intellectual disability. Has she even heard about it or read or seen other children with this condition, he muses. Maybe not. She has a very busy and successful career. This baby will change her life and turn everything upside down. Why did it have to be him that had to break the news to her? Why did it have to be Kamal to whom this happened? "Dear God" he prays softly to himself, as he looks at Kamal with compassion, "give me strength and give her courage."

But he walks calmly back to his table and sits down facing her. He smiles with professional ease but his brain is sifting through the many possibilities before him now. How should he tell her about her baby? Should he tell her at all? He could refer her to his friend, a psychologist, and let them handle this. He is seriously tempted to do this. Kamal sits there with a very definite sense of unease. Dr. Raut is behaving rather strangely today she thinks, even as she smiles back at him. He has not even examined the baby! But the vague fear she had when she came in is now intense and she feels it like a physical pain.

Dr. Raut feels frustrated and angry with himself because there is nothing really that he can do to help. So he is blunt. This surprises Kamal and she looks at him with a frown. Dr. Raut begins to speak before Kamal could ask any questions. "Kamal," he says, and without realizing it lowers his voice as he picks up paper clips from the table and slowly straightens them one by one. He is aware that he is talking faster than his usual easy going way but he has to say it before courage fails him. "Kamal," he begins again.

"Your son is intellectually disabled. It is something we call Downs Syndrome. We can only help you care for him because there is no cure for this. It is not a disease for which I can give you some medicine here. You must go to a specialist." He is repeating himself

7

but he feels he must make Kamal realize what now lay ahead of her. "The specialists will help you. Do you understand?"

Kamal looks at him with no sign of comprehension on her face. She smiles with uncertainty and the corner of her mouth twitches as if she is trying hard not to laugh outright at the strange things Dr. Raut was saying.

Dr. Raut tries again. "It is not your fault" he says, trying to talk as calmly and as professionally as possible and more in control of himself now. "It is nobody's fault. Sometimes things like this happen."

"Like what things happen?" thinks Kamal to herself.

Dr. Raut has a neat pile of straightened paper clips in front of him now. Now that he has said it, he expects the hopelessness that has weighed on him to lift a little. But he feels no different. He looks with a sense of utter helplessness at the sleeping child. He waits with ill-concealed anxiety for what he knows must come. Absolute stunned disbelief or heartrending, agonizing grief. He hates this. Really hates it. He wishes there were something he can do. Some words of wisdom to help her. He wishes that he could put his arms around her but of course he cannot do that, old friend though she is. So all he can do is to try to comfort her when she lets herself go in hysterical grief or screams and rants at him. He has experience of both. But strangely, Kamal does neither. Dr. Raut realizes that he is willing her to cry. Anything. Except sit so still and look at him with that strange smile on her face. If she did cry, he can call Nurse Coehlo and entrust her into her competent hands. But Kamal sits still and smiles her sweet smile.

Intellectually disabled? Disabled? Downs Syndrome? What on earth is he talking about? She does not understand what the doctor is saying. Her first thought is that Dr. Raut is trying to impress her, using strange sounding words. She is amused that after all these years he should resort to this. Using unintelligible medical jargon for what was perhaps a simple ailment is not like him, but then one never knew. These doctors, for all their degrees and professional 'so how are we today', also need an acknowledgement of their skills it seems. Just like other poor mortals with no specialist degrees. Kamal is amused.

But at the back of her head there is a consistent thought, nagging and refusing to be pushed away. Specialist? Did he say Specialist? Her Sunny needs a specialist? Now that was really funny. She lowers her head and hides her face behind Sunny in her lap and smiles in secret. She is a bit annoyed as well. Anyone can see that her baby is perfectly all right and perhaps needs just a little bit of tonic or something. So, what is all this about something called a syndrome?

So, smiling still and very calmly, she speaks slowly and carefully. "OK Doctor. If it is Downs Syndrome or whatever you called it, what medicines would you recommend? Is there something I can do at home? I can get someone to massage his legs. They are weak and that is why he cannot walk, you see. His brother walked when he was about nine months, I think, but this baby has been weak from birth and he has not been able to pick up strength and I am sure that if you prescribe some medicines, he will, will he? I MEAN WHAT MEDICINES CAN YOU RECOMMEND? There must be something somewhere. Something, somewhere for this... this... thing. What did you say it was called?" Her voice gradually becomes louder and she speaks hurriedly now, one sentence merging into the next as if she must speak as fast as possible. But even as she mouths the words she feels a heaviness settling on her shoulders and back and her legs seem to have become numb. She wants to get up and run out of the room. She feels nauseous. But she continues to sit there saying things she herself vaguely comprehends as foolish. She hears as if far away, someone's voice saying something unintelligible over and over again, little realizing that it is her own, until she finds herself, inexplicably in the arms of Nurse Coehlo.

All this while, Dr. Raut has sat in miserable silence. It is his experienced and compassionate nurse, Nurse Coelho, who coming in and taking in the situation with one practiced glance puts her motherly arms around Kamal and leads her gently out of the room making small soothing sounds. Kamal responds to the soft voice and to the soft motherly bosom which pillows her head. She gets a faint whiff of gardenia and ever after she will associate Nurse Coehlo with gardenia.

She sinks down on the settee in Nurse Coehlo's private domain and looks with incredulous eyes at the small child in her lap. This is Sunny. Her son. She knows something terrible has happened to him. She is only vaguely aware of what the doctor had said, refusing to acknowledge with her conscious mind what her unconscious had understood and known all along.

There is now absolute silence. Nurse Coehlo, back behind her desk is concerned for Kamal and it shows in her eyes and her face. She makes no attempts to intrude on Kamal's thoughts now. The moment is too private and too intense and belongs solely to Kamal. To cope with it or break under it. A clock ticks louder than usual. And somewhere outside in the rain-sodden garden a bird chirps happily.

Huddled on the settee, Kamal analyzes herself critically. She knows that what is happening to her is possibly a bout of hysteria. Never in all her life has she thought of herself as the hysterical type. But what the doctor had told her had somehow set her off. What had he said? Disabled. Intellectually disabled? Her Sunny disabled? And intellectually? What did it really mean? She wants to ask Nurse Coehlo about this. It is possible that the doctor has made a mistake. Everyone knew that nurses, especially experienced ones like Nurse Coehlo knew more than the doctors. But she feels drained and lethargic. She feels as if she will never talk again. At this moment she cannot bring herself to utter even a single word. Her brain refuses to function and a blankness settles on her, which mercifully spares her the cruelty of greater comprehension. It is only the thought that keeps flashing inside her head like an insistent neon sign that Dr. Raut may be wrong that helps her regain some measure of composure. She takes a long time though. A very long time.

Kamal, lying in bed now, remembers that it had taken many more visits and many months before she had even admitted to herself that her son, her Sunny, who could melt her strict husband to do the oddest things and could charm her to give him anything he wanted and laughed and looked at her with such twinkling eyes, was not normal. He had something called intellectual disability. He was something people called a child with Downs Syndrome.

CHAPTER III

Ajay was late home as well. A student of the Engineering College in Delhi, he often came home much after midnight. He went to his part time job straight from his classes. Often it would get very late because Ajay being a gregarious person needed to keep his social life alive. Living in South Delhi had its advantages but commuting to and from college was a nightmare. But it was only for another year and after that he should be on his own. This was a prospect that delighted him.

He saw that a light was still burning in his parents' bedroom. This worried him. Even though his father watched TV long into the night it was rarely later than midnight. His mother had always gone to bed as soon as dinner was over. He wondered what kept them awake.

Opening the front door softly, he stepped into the dark drawing room. With easy familiarity he found his way in to his own bedroom. Before he could even take off his warm jacket, he heard his mother call. Ajay responded immediately. "*Ji. Amma,*" he said and walked into his parents' bedroom. As he had expected his father sat watching TV. He looked at his father with a worried frown, which asked for an explanation of this unusual late night vigil. Their eyes met and in an unspoken mutual understanding he knew that he was being asked to be gentle with his mother. "What on earth could be wrong?" wondered Ajay. She was the stronger of the two. The disciplinarian who was definitely in charge of all family matters. But some things left her weak and defenseless. His younger brother Sunny was a prime cause. A swift charge of apprehension swept through him as he almost ran to her bedside. His mother looked drained and tired but smiled at him. With characteristic candor she came straight to the point. "Sunny has not come home," she said in a matter of fact way, as she held out her hand to Ajay. He grasped it, relief flooding him.

He smiled. "Is that all, *Amma*?" he said and sat on the side of her bed. "You had me worried." But he was irritated. It was almost always Sunny who reduced his mother to this state. What had he done now?

Kamal smiled a little tremulously at her first son. She held on to Ajay's hand trying to get some measure of assurance from him. She wanted him to say, "Don't worry *Amma*. I will go and bring him back." But Ajay said nothing. What indeed could he say? He sat looking at his mother with concern. Kamal turned her head away from Ajay so that he could not see the agony in her eyes. She nodded her head several times and let go of his hand.

Like his father, Ajay felt that perhaps his mother was unnecessarily worrying herself. Sunny will come home as he had several times before. He did not want to go out again this night. But she was rarely this upset. He was conscious of a slowly rising anger. It was always Sunny who could put his parents into a tizzy. Never him. Yes, he did realize that his brother needed their care and attention more than he did. He also felt a sense of guilt that it was Sunny and thank God, not he, who was intellectually disabled. Nevertheless, it irritated him when his parents expected him to look after Sunny. How was he to keep track of Sunny and what he did? It was wholly unreasonable. He said a little brusquely, "Oh. He will come back when he wants to, Amma. Has he not done so every time he was late?" He looked at his father and shook his head knowing that he would understand. He bent down and kissed the top of her head and went out of the room. He did not hear his mother say softly, "Never this late."

CHAPTER IV

Sunny stood outside the little restaurant in the Kailash market. The market was crowded this evening, as always. Naidu's, which Sunny haunted most evenings was where most of the student population in South Delhi hung out. Apart from being a fast food place it was much cheaper than the chicken and tikkas at the neighboring *dhabi*. Naidu's was not up-market at all and made no pretence of wanting to become one. It was small and clean but had an old world look. Thin bamboo matting, what was called '*pai*' back in Chennai, over the windows and over the one door gave it a laid back comfortable ambience. If it was reminiscent of a gently decaying club for the 'genteel folk' that had seen better days, it was because the furniture had been bought wholesale from the Anglo Indian Club, which had packed up when the man in charge had left Delhi. Green rattan chairs and circular tables with small bud vases made an attempt at decor but what came through overwhelmingly was the South Indian character of the restaurant. The aroma of *sambar* and chutney and *dosas* being fried proclaimed it for what it was.

Naidu, the owner was not much older than many of his clients. He was typically Dravidian with dark smooth skin and jet black hair. His height made him look lanky. Many of the girls who came to Naidu's had told him he looked like a film star. He smiled with genuine pleasure at these compliments, his white teeth against his dark skin making him all the more appealing. The person of Naidu himself was certainly one reason why Naidu's was so popular. But it was also his culinary skills. Naidu's mother had been a cook all her life. She would undertake to cook for affluent families when they wanted typically South Indian cuisine. She was well known in Chennai as one of the best and often had to turn down requests because she was over booked. Naidu remembered going along with her when he was just a small boy. He would sit in the kitchen and watch his mother as she began working. As he grew older he began to assist her and became so adept that very soon the families she cooked for would tell her to bring Naidu along. There came a time when he could not only cook better than his mother but also created his own recipes. Everyone, including Naidu himself knew that this was his life's vocation.

When his father died, his mother and he had come to Delhi. His mother who was fiercely ambitious for Naidu knew that with her son's culinary skills he should be where he would get maximum opportunity. It was she who had helped build up Naidu's. The special ambience the restaurant enjoyed was wholly due to Naidu himself. He had made it into a place which served a combination of student needs. A place to hang out, to meet girlfriends, or conduct serious discussions. Sometimes, and particularly during exam times, groups of students huddled around one of their more studious friends and listened to last minute explanations, or a masterly analysis of what questions to expect. At such times Naidu provided a continuous supply of cups of coffee or tea or cold drinks. His flair for empathizing with the young made him confidant, counselor, and keeper of secrets to a constantly changing clientele.

Naidu knew Sunny well. The first time he had come to Naidu's, he had just stood inside the door looking around apprehensively. He was trying to be like the others he saw around him. Hands in pockets and lounging around, Naidu had seen him come in and had watched him standing around for some time. He had made the first move. He walked up to Sunny and smiled at him. No prospective customer should hesitate coming in as this boy was doing. He saw straightaway that there was something strange about him. Slanting eyes, a snub nose and lanky hair but at the same time something charming. It was his innocent smile that got Naidu.

"Do you want something?" he had asked finally when no answers were forthcoming. He had not been prepared for the very honest answer.

"Yes. I want a coke" Sunny had said without a trace of inhibition. Naidu had wondered briefly whether to send him away. But a customer was a customer although this boy looked funny. But one had to be sure.

"Do you have the money for it?" Naidu had said quite unabashed at this insulting question, which intuition told him was to be asked.

Sunny had pulled out a hundred-rupee note and held it out waving it to and fro as if it was a flag. His action said, "What do you think of that." Then pushing past Naidu, he had sauntered across to one of the green rattan chairs and seated himself and had proclaimed loudly for everyone to hear, "I want one coke with a straw in it."

Naidu had laughed out aloud at this. He looked around to see if he was with someone. But no. He appeared to be totally on his own. He was a curious mixture of vulnerability and attempts at a show of confidence. It did not take Naidu long to figure out that his new customer was an innocent. Naidu served the boy himself. "One bottle of coke" said Naidu to Sunny "and one straw."

The pleasure on the boy's face had been obvious. Without wasting time he had straightaway started pulling on the straw oblivious to the people around him or to Naidu, who was watching him and waiting to see what he would do about his change for the hundred rupee note. But there had been no attempt at any further conversation.

"Don't you want your change?" Naidu had asked after a period of silence and for the second time that day felt unsure of how he should react.

"No," Sunny had said with a disarming smile. He added irrationally "My name is Sunny." A totally surprised Naidu had smiled back genially. He had leant over Sunny's table and tried to get him to talk. He had intuitively done what he had done a hundred times before whenever he sensed that one of the students in his restaurant needed that little bit of extra care. He was adept at it and this was the skill which the students who thronged there appreciated.

"Sunny, ha. So, you are alone Sunny? Where are your friends today?" Naidu had asked really wanting to know why he was alone. Sunny had looked at him and shrugged. "My friends are at home," he said. "Mummy, Daddy and *Bhaiya*." He had said this very matter of factly, without any emotion.

Mummy. Daddy and *Bhaiya*? These were his friends. So. Here was someone who was like a child. Who needed to be looked after. He knew without anyone telling him that this boy who called himself Sunny, would really never grow up. His heart warmed towards him. A strange and touching relationship began that day between Naidu and Sunny. It had become a very special bond. Who knows, Naidu had reasoned to himself, but for the grace of God, I could have been born like Sunny or my children, God bless them, could have been like Sunny?

Over the months Sunny had become a regular customer. Only Naidu knew how many of the cokes ordered by Sunny were on the house. He took care to keep a careful account of the hundred rupees Sunny had brought in the first day. Every waiter who served him knew how much of the advance was left and automatically deducted the day's quota whenever Sunny had come in. It had long since been used up. But for Sunny, the lack of money did not mean anything. On days when he had managed to get an odd rupee or two from his brother or father, he always promptly came up to pay. Often though, he came in and stood watching, but had the knowledge that today he should just sit quietly. Naidu would finally tell a waiter to serve him.
"OK give him a bottle of coke" he would say and "put a straw in it for him will you?" What impressed Naidu was the boy's dignity. He would never ask for a free drink and waited until he was asked. It was only the wide smile of genuine gratitude, which Sunny would flash across at him when he did get a drink that showed how desperately he had wanted one. Whenever this happened, Sunny would wend his way across the floor between tables to stand right in front of Naidu and say a loud but polite "Thank You." It embarrassed Naidu, especially when customers turned around to look at Sunny.

His usual reaction was a short *"Bas. Bas"* before turning away and pretending to be busy.

Today he watched Sunny come in and waved a hand at him. Sunny's face brightened. Being recognized made him so happy that he immediately came alive. He wanted to be like the others he saw around him, chatting and laughing. Part of a group. Not always on his own and always alone.

"Hi! *Yaar*," he said loudly to Naidu, waving his hand at him like some of the boys did when they came in. Naidu laughed and directed one of his waiters to serve Sunny. He was surprised to see Sunny turning to two young men who had been sitting quietly at a table near the door.

"Hi!" said Sunny to the two men who returned his greeting smilingly. Naidu's interest quickened. He continued to watch. Sunny's eyes were on the suave short man. There was no mistaking that this man was the leader of the twosome. Naidu knew he was called Rattan and the taller, darker one with pockmarks on his face was Bhima. Sunny seemed to be ridiculously happy to be with these two men and being part of the group.

How and when Sunny met these two men, wondered Naidu briefly. They were not the college crowd and not the business types either. But they had been coming into his restaurant very regularly for the past few weeks. They were no trouble at all. Good customers in fact. But Sunny with these two? Something made him uneasy but he could not put a finger on it. The three of them seemed to be getting on well. Extremely well in fact, thought Naidu, as Sunny guffawed loudly at something Bhima had said. At least they paid for Sunny's consumption of cokes. It was really not his business to pry but he could not help glancing occasionally at the table occupied by the odd group of three.

Sunny, meanwhile settled himself comfortably in one of the green rattan chairs. "Thank You" he said politely with a grin at Rattan, when a plate of pakoras was placed in front of him. Both Rattan and Bhima laughed at this and thought it funny. It seemed to be Sunny's favorite word. He said it in his characteristic way with a lopsided grin and his head slanted to one side. Rattan nodded his head slightly to indicate to Bhima that ordering pakoras for Sunny had been the right thing to do and was approved.

"So, Sunny" said Rattan, watching the rapidly disappearing coke, which Sunny sipped straight from the bottle with gusto.

"What did you do today?"

"Went to school."

"And?" prompted Bhima.

"Nothing" said Sunny and repeated, "Went to school."

There was no doubting the boredom which school inspired in him. Sunny went to a Special School where he was taught what the school called 'functional academics'. Recognizing the alphabets, writing his name, matching colors and similar activities, all of which were designed to improve his skills in what society considered to be necessary if one wanted to be a part of it. Most of the time however, he made paper bags. Good strong ones. Fold the sheet of paper lengthwise, turn up the bottom and paste. Fold over the side and paste again. Fold and paste, fold and paste, always the same, every single day. He did it mechanically now and it meant nothing to him. The only excitement was when someone tipped over the pot of paste and there was a mess on the floor or when the paper stacked in a corner got soaked with water because it was too close to the water cooler and it had dripped for hours before the teacher noticed it. At such times there was a happy flurry of activity. Teacher would say "Take out everything into the yard under the hot sun." "Wipe the floor." "Shift the tables and chairs." What Sunny enjoyed most of all was being told to keep the other children quiet and to help out. It was always Sunny who got the cleaning-up jobs. The teachers knew he would do a thorough job.

But if someone had asked Sunny what he wanted to do, he would have most definitely opted for something he could have done outdoors. Maybe pottering around in the school garden, watering the plants, sitting under the trees with the *malis* at lunch, smoking a *beedi* perhaps and generally being left alone. He would have made an excellent *mali* too because he loved working with his hands and everything that went into the upkeep of a garden. When there were flowers in the garden, he spent hours looking at them and touching them and one could have sworn that when he talked to them they did respond and only Sunny could understand the strange and wonderful things they told him. He did this at home too, with his mother watching him indulgently, telling him what to do. But no one had ever asked Sunny what he wanted to do. His companions in school were like him. With different degrees and kinds of intellectual disability. But mostly they were a happy lot and enjoyed being together. They did what they were asked to do, if they could do it. If not, they just sat around until the hard worked teacher came around to help.

Of course Sunny was much happier in Naidu's. It had a kind of happy grown up atmosphere where everyone sat in groups with their friends and there was always talk and laughter. Whenever Sunny was with Rattan and Bhima he felt as if it was an important event. It had come to hold a special fascination for him. He knew he was welcome here. His new friends would listen to him with interest. He could talk to them and say whatever was in his mind. They never corrected or reprimanded him. He was like all the others around him. With Rattan egging him on now, he had no difficulty in talking about what was uppermost in his mind.

"My mother said I must not take her money," he said. In the evening there had been an incident, which left Sunny, confused and hurt. He did not like it when his mother looked stern and her voice became angry. He had attempted to open his mother's handbag to take out some money. He knew that if he wanted to buy things he needed a wallet and in the wallet should be some coins and some paper money, just like his *Bhaiya*. Perhaps a photograph as well but he had not figured out whose. He knew that his mother's handbag had both kinds of money and it was always there. This was the place from where he could get money whenever he wanted. He had learnt to be cautious and stealthy because he was well aware that he was doing what he had been told not to do.

Did Sunny ever realize that he was stealing? It was hard to tell. Kamal thought that she had instilled a fear of consequences in Sunny if he ever stole anything. But Sunny did not understand the taboo on stealing. Today, even though he knew that his mother did not want him to take the money out of her bag, his need to get out and find congenial company was so great that he had actually hunted for his mother's handbag and had it open in his hand when she had come in. Kamal rarely allowed anger to surface. Especially with Sunny. But when she saw him actually stealing money, stealing like a common thief, a long suppressed fear took hold of her.

"SUNNY. PUT THAT DOWN AT ONCE. AT ONCE." Anger made her voice shrill and her breath came in gasps. She took Sunny by the arm and shook him fiercely.

"Never. Never. Never take money out of my bag again, Sunny," she said, shaking him by the arm with each word she said.

"Do you understand?" "Do you?" she shouted.

Sunny did certainly understand her anger. He knew it was not right. You should not take things, which did not belong to you. He knew all that. But what did you do when you wanted some money? The money was his mother's. He knew that too. It did not occur to him that he could have simply asked for some money. His mother had given him money sometimes. But this time, somehow, he had just thought that he could take it himself. His mother's anger frightened him and he had run out of the house. She had made such an impact on him that he remembered it even now. All he had wanted was money. He could not understand why he could not get the money he wanted just like *Bhaiya* did. So, it had been in a rather somber mood that he had come to Naidu's. Meeting his friends had already elevated his spirits. He was more than ready to talk to them.

Rattan saw that Sunny was not in his usual jovial mood and guessed correctly that there had been some unpleasantness at home. His remark about his mother told him a lot. He was concerned. Was it possible that the boy was in some kind of trouble?

"Why do you want money Sunny *bhai*?" he asked.

Sunny was forthright. "I want to come here everyday and have a coke."

Rattan was relieved. So it was not a major problem at all. He laughed loudly; head thrown back and then smiled hugely at Bhima. He then made a fist and put it on his closed mouth and nodded his head several times. Both the smile and this gesture was something which Bhima had learnt to interpret. It meant that Rattan was thinking and that he would take over now. If anyone disturbed him now it was at his own peril.

Rattan had been watching Sunny. A slow smile spread over his face. "No problem" said Rattan now to Sunny. He pulled out a ten rupee note. "Take this, take this" he continued pushing the note into Sunny's hand and closing his fingers over it. He knew exactly how to win Sunny's confidence.

"This is for you. Sunny *bhai*, ask me if you want anything. You understand? Anything. No money? And this has upset you? *Arre bhai*. Ask me anytime." He smiled at Sunny and casually put his arm across Sunny's shoulders. Then turning to the waiter, who happened to be passing by, he said with a laugh. "*Yaar*. Listen. Treat this boy well. He is Rattan's friend now." Sunny smiled radiantly nodding his head up and down in acknowledgement making the waiter smile in response.

"Yes. *Yaar*" he said loudly and shaking his head in the characteristic way he had when he was happy. "I am Rattan's friend." When everyone around him laughed he was blissfully content. He had made his friends laugh. He felt a sense of achievement. His mother's anger and his own upset was fast disappearing from his mind. Naidu turned at the sound of the laughter. What goes on here, he wondered again briefly, before he was called away by one of the other customers.

If only Kamal knew that Sunny was enjoying himself in the little restaurant in the local market, her life and that of Sunny would have taken wholly different directions. But Sunny not coming home for dinner and bursting in just when she began to get worried had happened so many times that she waited. Waiting for Sunny had become a practiced skill.

CHAPTER V

Rattan and Bhima had met in Naidu's exactly three weeks earlier. Bhima's pock marked face made him look ferocious but he was the milder of the two. The name Bhima did not suit him at all. He was thin to the point of being scrawny. Dark in complexion and with hair oiled to slickness and combed back, he was anything but a *Bhima*, and synonymous with strength. Rattan on the other hand was short but muscular. At one time he had been the champion wrestler in his village before Delhi had lured him to its bright lights. If a film scout had spotted him in his youth he could have become a film star. In fact, this was one reason for Rattan's disgruntlement. He was handsome. He had a wonderful body. What use had it been to him except a few hours when he indulged himself with women who came willingly to him in the many villages, which he had visited? Even here, in the big city of Delhi, he had sensed the educated city women looking at him in that certain way. It amused him. But with no schooling, no job and no one to look out for him, Rattan had been forced to set himself up in the kind of business he knew best. Masterminding small burglaries.

He was the one with all the bright ideas. Until he had met Bhima most of these ideas had remained locked up in his mind for he could not talk about them to anyone. He was also very lazy. He was happy if someone could put his plans into action and he got his share out of it.

One ill-fated night after committing a petty theft he had almost got caught. The goddess of luck who was always with him had deserted him that night. It had not been a major job either. The house was one of many in an apartment block. In spite of lights on the landing and lights inside the house, Rattan had known that Flat A12 was temporarily unoccupied. The family had left just a day ago and he had known with an instinct born out of practice that if he did not finish the job soon, the opportunity would go. He had climbed the stairs nimbly as if he lived in one of the flats. Anyone seeing him would never doubt that he knew where he was going. Indeed he did. Flat A12. He switched off the landing lights. Okay. It is fused and that is what everyone will think he told himself. Pulling out his small slim torch he expertly picked the lock. Delhi was full of locks like this one and he was surprised that the owners had not thought to put in more security gadgets. Well. It was not for him to complain. Once inside, an efficient and practiced search yielded sufficient for a month or two. An expensive clock, obviously imported, suits and saris hanging in the cupboard, which again was locked with a flimsy contraption he flicked open with one twist of his small knife. "Enough," said a small voice inside him. Rattan knew it was his goddess warning him to stop but he hesitated, undecided, whether he should take just one more look around. That was his undoing, because it was these few seconds of indecision, which had messed up his whole evening.

As he stepped out softly and closed the door he saw with dismay that a man whom he recognized as the servant who worked in A12 was coming up the stairs. Rattan panicked. What was this man doing here? He was supposed to be in his village and the family away for a week at least. He did something very foolish. He began to run down the stairs. He realized even as he ran that the servant would not have known anything until he had actually gone up to the flat and found it unlocked. The lights had remained switched off. But it was this sudden taking to his heels that had alerted the servant. He shouted and started to follow Rattan taking two steps at a time down the stairs. Thanks to the darkness outside and his knowledge of the locality, Rattan had shaken off the servant smartly. He had run down the stairs and up the stairs of the block immediately next to it. He kept going all the way to the terrace and stopped there, panting and cursing himself for being such a fool. Peering over the edge of the terrace wall he saw the man go shouting down the lane. But caution prevailed and he stayed put. He was to thank his intuition for very soon the servant was back, but this time there was a small crowd around him. Crouched on the rooftop, Rattan could hear him talking to the family in the next flat. The police must be informed said a man's voice and a woman's voice agreed shrilly. "And hurry up," she said. "The man may be hiding here for all you know." "How right you are lady," said Rattan to himself with a smile. He had regained his usual composure by this time. He even guessed what the man would say. He was right. The husband, it must be the husband mustn't it, had said patronizingly, "Don't be silly Rina and don't worry. The man must have run for his life as soon as he saw Bahadur coming up the stairs." Rattan sent a mock salute towards the unknown man.

It took about an hour and a half for all the excitement to finish and the people to get back into their houses and lock and bolt their doors. Once he was sure that there was to be no more excitement, Rattan came smartly down the stairs once again. No one saw him. Everyone was safe inside. The servant of A12 no doubt lamenting the fact that it was his flat that had been burgled.

But it had been a nerve racking experience and had left him with a desperate need to find someone who would take the kind of risks he had to take. It was only his superior skill in dodging traffic and selecting sure avenues of escape that had prevented his being caught that day. He knew that the servant had not been able to get a really good look at him and that he would not be recognized even if he went back to the same locality, but it was good policy not to push your luck. The small burglaries, which he had been doing for the past five years suited him. But he could do without the risks, thank you. Identifying where and when to strike, planning even the most insignificant of details, a talent for giving the smallest of jobs the same careful considerations as he did to more profitable efforts and most of all the ability to intuitively know when to lay off. These were the very special skills that had been his from birth.

The most ideal situation, he always thought, would be to continue the business but let someone else take the risks. Thinking about this excited him. If only he could find someone who would be willing to carry out his plan for a price, he could do the superb planning he knew he could and sit back to enjoy the rewards.

His favorite reminiscence was the burglary he had committed in East Delhi. The police were looking for a man with a limp. Rattan smiled in delight thinking about the way he had managed that. Now, safe in South Delhi, he needed to begin some work again. Funds were getting low and he had started visiting Naidu's with the specific purpose of gathering some information. But first he had to establish himself. That took time and careful day to day observations. Who went where? Who frequented which restaurant at what time? What timings did the families he had mentally listed as 'most profitable' keep aside for their work, their entertainment? Children? How old? Which schools or colleges? It was a lot of hard work and a lot of legwork as well to do the kind of expert survey he needed.

He had continued to come to Naidu's more for a place to come to than with any real hope of finding an accomplice. It had not been until his fourth visit that he had met Bhima. He seemed to be a regular too but something about him made Rattan wary. On a crowded day when Naidu's was swarming with students who were coming in from evening classes and pre-term exams, Naidu had asked if he could seat another customer at his table. A dark pock marked man had joined Rattan. They had looked at each other and an embarrassed silence followed, like when two people are perfectly willing to be nice to each other but don't know how to begin.

"From Delhi?" Rattan had asked finally after both men had tried to avoid each other's eyes a couple of times.

"*Arre.* No. I am from Rajasthan," Bhima had answered letting down his guard now that verbal contact had been made. He went on without being prompted. "I am looking for some spare parts to take back to my village."

Rattan knew with a certainty born of long experience that the man sitting in front of him was no more a spare parts dealer than he was. His pulse quickened with interest. But he had to be certain.

"Rajasthan? I have been there several times. Which part of Rajasthan?" Rattan continued.

Bhima laughed. "Nowhere you would know. It is a very small village" he said. Then he added, "It is almost near the desert. The very end you know." He looked intently at Rattan as he said this.

Rattan's interest flared. He felt compelled to keep asking questions. It was his goddess guiding him. If he asked the questions he had in mind he may risk angering this man at his table. On the other hand he may not, if his suspicions were correct. He took the risk.

He chuckled and shook his head sideways in disbelief. He said, almost rudely, "In a village in Rajasthan? Spare parts? For what - bullock carts?" His voice indicated that he did not believe what he had heard. But Bhima had not taken offence. In fact, he had agreed.

"Yes" he had said with a smile. "For bullock carts. You may not believe it, but rubberized wheels are the latest *bhai*. And of course there is always a need for spare parts for tractors."

Rattan and Bhima looked at each other. Then Bhima's smile widened. "In fact," he went on, "anything at all that I feel will sell in the village."

"Ah," said Rattan with complete understanding. He smiled in acceptance of Bhima's statement and a gracious nod of his head. But the persistent clamor in his mind, which said "Watch out for this man" was not to be ignored. He was almost sure that this man was also on the look out for something. "What? Why? Was he perhaps his man? Was he a petty burglar like himself?" What a curious hand fate had dealt him, if it turned out that this man would be the one to help him finally achieve the life of leisure and minimum risks that was his dream. And he had actually come straight to his table! At this thought Rattan threw back his head and laughed out loudly. A surprised Bhima smiled. Their eyes locked and in a strange and silent exchange of communication each acknowledged the other's possible support in their respective ventures.

CHAPTER VI

This had been the beginning. Over the weeks both of them had realized that if they teamed up, they could make a very profitable partnership. Rattan was sure that at last he might have the man who would be able to understand his plans and carry them out the way he wanted. He was not an impulsive man. Everything had to be weighed for its impact and consequences and then action taken. But sometimes, as now, some inner voice, which he liked to tell himself, was his own personal goddess told him that this was his chance. He should go ahead with courage. Now, sitting with both Bhima and Sunny, Rattan's mind was racing with different plans. He had sitting with him at his table, the only two people in the world who were the means to a perfect solution. To a life of leisure and big money. This pock faced man who called himself Bhima and this boy who was so guileless that it would be easy to get him to do whatever he wanted. What kind of a plan would make use of both Bhima and Sunny? Bhima's unquestioning acceptance of his orders and the innocence of this boy. He smiled.

Rattan believed in fate. The cards fate dealt him were to be taken as challenges to be worked out. Opportunities were meant to be taken and if one did not make the most of them, then it was one's own fault. The meeting with Sunny had been one such opportunity. In fact Sunny and his innocent and vulnerable charm had made him change his plans but now they were even better.

Life was good. He ordered a second drink for Sunny. Bhima smiled but said nothing. He was content to leave things to Rattan. Ever since the day when he had first sat down at Rattan's table things had developed swiftly. From an initial suspicion and ingrained wariness of all strangers, Bhima had come to realize that in Rattan he had found the support he needed. He was willing and ready to leave all the planning to Rattan as long as he got a share.

Naidu continued to watch the trio on and off. The thought of Sunny with these two men made him uneasy though he could not say why. He knew that Sunny had met the two men in his restaurant, and as long as they were not creating problems for him, he should really let them be. When Sunny had finished his second drink and demolished a plate of paneer pakoras, Rattan said casually, "Sunny *bhai.* Would you like to come with Bhima and me tonight?" Bhima sat up, suddenly alert and looked fixedly at Rattan. Sunny's immediate reaction was one of happiness.

"Yes. Yes. Yes" he said, nodding his head up and down. "Yes."

"Where would you like to go Sunny?"

Sunny knew exactly where he wanted to go. "To the temple," he said.

"Why the temple?" asked a surprised Bhima.

"To collect the marigold flowers there and take them home."

This was something new they had not heard before. If Sunny went to the temple people there obviously knew who he was. Rattan pursed his lips thoughtfully. It would never do to accompany Sunny to the temple. But he had to learn more.

"Oh. I see. Do you go there often?" said Rattan with genuine interest.

Sunny was happy to talk. "Yes. The uncle there allows me to clean up the courtyard and then he lets me take the flowers home," he explained. He wanted to tell his new friends all about the temple. Bhima and Rattan listened with interest. So the boy did go to other places as well. Rattan was concerned with one thing. Sunny's answer would tell him what to do.

"Does anyone know you go to the temple," asked Rattan.

Sunny was not too sure. "I don't know," he said hesitantly. If he did not know would this nice man get angry with him?

But Rattan was only trying to gauge how he could use this new information Sunny had given him. He put his folded arms on the table and leant towards Sunny. He said softly "Your mother?"

"Yes," said Sunny at once and then "I don't know." Rattan smiled slightly and shook his head at an irritated Bhima. The again more definitely this time he said "Yes. *Amma* knows I go to the temple."
Rattan continued "Your father?"
Sunny was sure. "No" he said firmly.

Rattan leant back in his chair and smiled at Sunny. His mind was made up. Tonight was the night. He had a grateful and happy Sunny and an alert and faithful accomplice. He had cased one of the houses in the neighborhood and had kept careful watch for the past two weeks. That would be his destination now. Besides, once he made up his mind, it was bad luck to change plans. He got up and put his arms around Sunny. A slight tilt of his head said "Let's get out." His eyes told Bhima that the time had come to put into action what they had been planning for weeks. A delighted Sunny jumped up to put his own arm over Rattan's shoulder. This was his friend. He was going with him to the temple. Just like the people who came into the restaurant, he was also going away with his friends. To Sunny, Rattan was everything that he had ever wanted. Brother, friend, confidant and counselor in turn. Sunny would have done anything for Rattan. When he was asked if he would like to come with them to the temple, he did not hesitate. He knew vaguely that his mother and father would wait. They would keep his dinner ready on the table. But Sunny lacked the capacity to judge the situation. He knew that in the temple there would be *bhajans*, and lots of garlands. He loved ringing the shiny brass bell that hung in the courtyard and when he went home he could carry armloads of marigold garlands; these he could add to the drying collection back home in his room on the first floor. He knew that his mother often had to come up to clean his room and took away the dried and drying garlands. He liked

32

arranging them around the photographs and pictures he had collected.

These collections of pictures spanning a truly representative selection of religion, politics and sex, adorned the walls of Sunny's room on the terrace of his house. A picture of Lord Krishna fought for space with a peeling photograph of a nymphet bathing under a gushing waterfall. Christ looked on benignly with a hand raised in blessing. The latest heart throb of a successful Hindi film stood looking menacingly at the world, hands on hips. Overseeing all of them was a toothless Gandhi, smiling as if in approval of a world without discrimination at last. To Sunny, they were all the same. Each one of the pictures had evoked in him feelings which made him feel good. He liked his pictures. Now his friends were going to help him take home the bright marigold garlands he liked so much. They were nice people. He liked them too.

Never in all his life had had had anyone invited him to accompany them. He felt immensely pleased and though he could not articulate what he felt or analyze why he felt this way, it was just the sheer satisfaction of being needed by another human being. The happiness that comes with a sense of belonging to someone. Sunny was now a part of the Rattan-Bhima set up. The jaunty spring in his step and the ever ready laughter with which he greeted even the most causal remarks of Rattan told their own story. Sunny went out of the restaurant with his friends. He raised his hand in salute to Naidu.

"We are going to the temple," he said loudly for all to hear.

Nice. Very nice thought Rattan. Sunny had unwittingly approved the plan he had in mind.

CHAPTER VII

At Naidu's it had been a busy day as usual. Now the restaurant was silent and the workers were cleaning up before going home. Naidu came out and lit his cigarette. He moved his shoulders trying to get rid of the tiredness. He inhaled deeply and sighed. It was a sigh of satisfaction. It had been a profitable day. He turned to go back inside, his mind busy with a new lentil and peanut concoction he had been reading about. A shout startled him and he saw a man walking purposefully towards him. He stopped in surprise. Who would want to see him at this time of the night? It was past midnight. He tensed. His first reaction was one of fear. It was a genuine fear, which had always lurked at the back of his mind that someday he would be robbed or worse. But this man was alone. So he waited.

The man who came up to him was small framed and certainly didn't look as if he could rob anybody. He was breathing in an agitated sort of way which was caused as much by his fast walk as by the turmoil going on in his mind. It was Sunny's father.

Prem had decided to look for Sunny in the restaurant where he knew Sunny spent a greater part of every evening. He came straight to what he wanted to say. "My son comes here every day," he began. "He is disabled. I mean he is not like other kids his age. You see he is twenty three years old but he has a… a… a something which will never make him what people call normal. The thing is have you seen him?"

Naidu knew at once that he was referring to Sunny. "You mean Sunny?" he asked smiling.

"Yes. Yes" said an eager Prem coming closer to Naidu so that he could get a better look at his face. "Have you seen Sunny today?"

"Why yes," said Naidu taken aback. "I did see him here in the morning and again in the afternoon. Why? What is the matter?"

But Prem had already turned to go. He had a nauseous feeling in his stomach and his heart thumped with fear. He knew for a certainty

34

that this time it was not a simple matter of Sunny coming home late. Something had happened. But what? He could not bring himself to tell this man about Sunny. He wanted to get away and rush home. He would tell Kamal and they would figure out what to do now. So he turned abruptly even as a genuinely concerned Naidu put out a restraining hand.

He called out to the retreating figure "He went to the temple with his two friends." Prem stopped abruptly and came back to Naidu.

"His two friends?" he said, his voice quivering. "Who were they? Do you know them? When did they go?"

Naidu was concerned. "Sunny knew these two men," he said trying to calm this man in front of him. "Are you Sunny's father, Sir?" he said respectfully now.

But Prem did not answer. He stood as if he could not walk again. Sunny with two strange men. Sunny's friends. How well he knew Sunny's need for friends. Temple. The man said Sunny had gone to the temple. He knew the temple Sunny frequented. So, he was safe after all. He was at the temple. He grabbed hold of Naidu's arms with both his hands. When he spoke again, his voice was choked with emotion. "Thank you" he said. "Thank you." His mind would insist on seeing visions of Sunny bursting in on them in the morning. It said, he is not lost after all. Only delayed. Yes. Only delayed.

"You see," he explained to Naidu. "We thought Sunny was lost. But now I will look for him at the temple." Naidu watched Sunny's father walk away with apprehension. He mouthed a silent prayer. "Sunny, please go home. Please go home."

35

CHAPTER VIII

Sunny was tired. He had walked a long way. Rattan was taking no chances. He wanted no one to see Sunny. It was easy to remember him since he looked and acted so peculiar. But they did arrive finally at a house, which looked as if no one lived there. There was not even a single light. Sunny commented on this at once. It did not occur to him to ask why they had not gone to the temple as he had expected but had come instead to someone's house. His trust in Rattan was complete.

"There is no electricity," he said.

"I know," said Rattan. But even as he said it, he turned it into the perfect explanation for what he had to do.

"Sunny" he continued, "We will go in first and fix the lights. You stand out here near the gate. We will call you in when we are ready." This would give them time to call the *chowkidar* who was supposedly awake and guarding the house and deal with him. If any one saw Sunny standing outside and questioned him, he was ready to abandon Sunny there and disappear.

"Will we go to the temple after this?" asked Sunny surprising both Rattan and Bhima.

"Of course. Of course" said Rattan. "But Bhima and I have to go away for a few days and we have to do some packing first and then to the temple." Sunny understood this. This was Rattan's house. His mother also went to the temple before going away on one of her many trips on work. He obediently stood just outside the gate.

Rattan and Bhima stepped softly through the gate, which they left open. Rattan rang the bell. Two longs and one short jab. Rattan's careful study had informed him that the *chowkidar* instead of patrolling the house after dark ensconced himself comfortably in his master's chair and watched movie after movie on the cable network.

The maid went home at 4.00 p.m. though on occasion Rattan had seen her leave much later. But she never spent the night. So, the *chowkidar* left to his own fancies was usually sound asleep at this time of night. It was exactly 12.00 midnight. An auspicious hour thought Rattan.

As Rattan had known, the *chowkidar* was sound asleep stretched out on his master's cot in the bedroom. The ringing of the bell woke him up with a start but it took him some time to heave himself out of bed and stagger with sleep dimmed eyes to the front door. "Who is it?" he asked though the door. A voice announced that an urgent letter had come by courier. This satisfied him. It was his duty to collect all letters and send them on to his employer's office every second day. A couriered letter meant urgent. Yawning hugely, he opened the door just a wee bit to identify the caller. Suddenly he found himself yanked violently forward from the doorway and thrown down on to the ground. He saw a dim figure standing in front of him. But this was just before he felt the blow on his head from behind and lost consciousness.

It had all been meticulously planned. A straightforward plan which would work because of its very simplicity. Bhima had been fast and sure. A swift hard blow and the *chowkidar* was carried inside and put on the bed in his master's luxurious bedroom where he had already been sleeping. Rattan covered him with the thin quilt lying at the foot of the bed, making Bhima laugh soundlessly.

All this while Sunny stood obediently where he had been asked to stand, just outside the gate. If any one saw him standing there they would not suspect a thing. Even if someone did ask him questions, both Rattan and Bhima knew that Sunny would confuse them so much with what he knew, combined with what little he remembered that no one could get anything worthwhile out of him.

"The best thing about Sunny *bhai*," as Bhima was to say later, "is that his memories of what happened will become so dim that even if the police question him he will have a different version everyday." Meeting Sunny was a rare stroke of luck.

The *chowkidar* taken care of, Bhima materialized suddenly beside Sunny, like a wraith in the diffused light of a street lamp, which kept flickering on and off. He whispered, "Close the gate before you come in."

Bhima took him by the arm. "We want you to help us do some packing Sunny." He kept to what Rattan had said. Sunny was obedient. He quietly shut the gate behind him. He was delighted. He was being allowed to actually help them. He knew all about packing clothes. He always helped his mother to pack her things in the brown suitcase every time she went away on one of her trips. He nodded his head in assent with his lopsided grin lost in the darkness of that quiet and still house.

No thoughts of the peculiar behavior of his friends plagued him. The whispering, the instructions to be quiet and stand still and the utter darkness inside the house when they stepped in. He was content to keep close to Bhima and do as he was told. If a vague and unexplained uneasiness made a momentary appearance it vanished as soon as Rattan came in from one of the back rooms, a torchlight bobbing up and down in his hands. He came forward and put a friendly arm over Sunny's shoulders.

Copying the whispering of both Bhima and Rattan, Sunny pointed to the torch in Rattan's hands.

"*Bhaiya*, is the electricity not come yet?"

It was Rattan who was surprised now. So Sunny did remember. Sometimes.

But now he said "No electricity" and cursed under his breath about the city's electric supply. This sounded familiar to Sunny. His father sometimes said similar things when the electricity failed.

"My father also says the same thing," he said trying to focus his eyes on Rattan. There was a smothered laugh from Bhima behind him.

But Sunny had already lost interest in the conversation. He squinted at a small portable radio cassette player perched on a side table. It looked expensive and sleek. It looked very much like the one his *bhaiya* had at home. Rattan's torch picked it out from among the shadows, which surrounded it.

"Ooooh" said Sunny in appreciation. Rattan nonchalantly propelled Sunny towards it.

"Do you like it" he asked. "Take it if you do."

Sunny hesitated. Take the radio cassette player? Something he had wanted for a long time. He looked uncertainly at Rattan narrowing his eyes to see in the dark.

"It is alright," said Rattan. "It is mine and I want to give it to you for helping us tonight. Take this and then whatever you think we should take for our journey. What ever you think is interesting. You can start with this radio cassette player I picked up from Japan."

Japan made no sense to Sunny. Told to take the radio cassette player certainly did. He set about avidly looking for other interesting things, shining the torch he had been given haphazardly from floor to ceiling and back again, making a nervous Bhima whisper loudly in his ear more than once to keep the torch on the ground. "ON THE GROUND. Do you understand?"

"OK. OK." said an exasperated Sunny and nodded in the dark. Of course he understood. He had to take things which he liked and give it to Rattan to take on his trip just like he handed his mother the things she asked him to when she went on a trip.

Busy with flashing the torch around to locate the things he wanted Sunny did not notice that both Rattan and Bhima had left him in the drawing room. They were both busy in the bedrooms. He felt no fear at being in a dark house. He could clearly hear his friends inside talking in whispers. Sunny knew that Bhima and Rattan were also busy packing.

Sunny stayed in the drawing room and leisurely looked around exclaiming loudly about some of the things he saw. There were many paintings on the wall and small exquisite handicraft items collected from different countries for the owners fancied them selves as connoisseurs of art. It was a beautifully kept well-furnished single unit house with a little narrow lawn in front. It had an exit at the back, opening on to the service lane. This had been one of the reasons that Rattan had decided it would be a safe bet. Even if Sunny mucked things up for them, they could always escape from the back and leave him out in front.

Sunny was finding it difficult to select things to take. He liked the figure of a dancing doll on the table. It swayed when you touched it. He hesitated before taking it but finally did succumb to his liking for it. Meanwhile, Rattan and Bhima working swiftly had collected cash and clothes. With the *chowkidar* snoring gently on the bed, they opened cupboards expertly and took out all the costly silk saris. These were always in demand and were easy to get rid of. Disappointingly there was not much jewelry but the cash, which they found in between the saris was substantial and Rattan felt their efforts had been worthwhile. Thanks to the woman of the house for keeping so much money hidden away from her husband thought Rattan with amusement.

When they were finally ready to leave they discussed briefly how to get Sunny out of the house. They had thought of leaving him there for the *chowkidar* to deal with when he came to. But when the time came it had been ridiculously easy.

"We have to lock up," said Rattan. "These days you never know when thieves will burgle your house." Sunny nodded in complete agreement and Bhima with difficulty choked back the laughter which threatened to come guffawing out any minute. Sunny walked out with the radio cassette player and the doll clutched in his hands.

"Wait for us outside the gate Sunny *bhai*" said Bhima. "We have to close the door and lock it."

Letting Sunny go out first had been deliberate. The silence told them it was safe to venture out now. Rattan peered cautiously with his head just outside the gate. Much to his own surprise he felt a twinge of remorse. Sunny was a picture of patience, waiting like a little child for its mother, he thought and cursed. For some strange reason, and he felt uncomfortable. "I wish he had taken off," he thought, but of course Sunny would never do anything without being told. He latched the gate and put his arm over Sunny's shoulder knowing that Sunny enjoyed this little token of affection. He hesitated now, debating the next step. The plan had been to knock Sunny out as they had done with the *chowkidar*. But now Rattan put a restraining hand on Bhima. A jittery Bhima turned around in astonishment. Rattan ignored him.

"No." It was a firm order and even as he said it he knew he was not acting wisely. In fact he was allowing himself to become sentimental about this boy. What was wrong with him? The choicest of curses muttered softly did nothing to lessen his hesitation. This boy would never know what had happened here tonight nor would he be able to give any explanations. He did not want to hurt Sunny. He was getting soft. But all he said was "Sunny. Wait here. We will come back for you."

Sunny did not like this idea of being asked to wait and left behind all by himself. He wanted to be with Rattan. He felt a vague fear. He realized that it was very late at night. He knew he should not be out so late. His mother would be angry again. So he took hold of Rattan by the arm. "I want to come with you," he said. "I do not want to stay here alone."

Bhima, already at pains to leave the scene of their crime reacted with savage anger. Sunny, with his back to Bhima, never knew what had hit him. As he fell to the ground, his one thought was to save the radio cassette player and he held it close to his chest and fell with it in a small crumpled heap on to the soft soil. The dancing doll fell miraculously on its feet and the motion set it swaying its hips wildly.

Rattan made a movement to stop Bhima but he was too late. He was furious. This was not to have happened. He had realized that Sunny safe back in his home could be used again. It was this thought as well as an increasingly uncomfortable liking for Sunny that had made him change his earlier plan to knock Sunny out and leave him there. But left at the gate he would have waited patiently for the car, which would never have come. The *chowkidar* would have found him or a passer by. Now he would never know what Sunny would do when he came to. Rattan did not like uncertainties. He started to walk away when Sunny made motions of sitting up and groaned loudly.

"Mummy" he sobbed, "Mummy." Rattan quickly jumped behind the tree that bordered the road. He could not risk having Sunny see him now and perhaps break out into loud crying. He had to wait and see what Sunny would do. He could not still the concern which unbidden reared itself in his mind. He was really angry with Bhima, who aware that he had made a serious error stood by quietly with the heavy suitcase pulling down his shoulder and making him look strange and deformed in the half-light.

Sunny was only aware of one thing now. The pain in his head. He was lying on the ground a little distance away from what he thought was Rattan and Bhima's house. There was no sign of his friends now. He did not even begin to analyze how or why he was lying on the ground. He did remember going with Rattan and Bhima into their house. He remembered helping them to pack some of the belongings they had wanted for their journey. They were going in a train to a far away place. He wanted to go too but they said they would come back for him. He was used to being told to wait. But the house was now dark and silent. He had no idea what time it was. His head throbbed. He felt cold and afraid. He was in a strange place he did not recognize. The pain made him think of his mother. He knew that at home he could tell his mother about the pain in his head and she would make it all right. So, he had to get home soon. Most of all he did remember with bewilderment that something had hit him on the head. It was something he could not understand.

With effort he stood up and started walking towards what he thought was the way home. Sobbing loudly now confused and with a rapidly swelling concussion on the side of his head, he stumbled on and did not see his two friends, Rattan and Bhima, standing in the shadows watching him. Bhima was not too sure they should let him go. Let us take him with us, he urged Rattan. But Rattan would only shake his head. He smiled when he saw Sunny get up and realized that he was actually relieved that Sunny was not too seriously hurt. All that he would be left with was a sore head. The boy had done excellent work tonight. Implicit obedience and no questions asked. He would definitely be useful someday again. As Rattan and Bhima watched Sunny get up and stagger away down the road, Rattan was happy with the way things had turned out in spite of the wholly unprovoked and unplanned action of Bhima. He smiled, nodding in satisfaction. They knew where to find him.

"Well" he said, when Sunny was out of sight. He turned angrily towards Bhima "It worked out alright in the end in spite of your stupid hitting out at Sunny. I do not know what comes over you sometimes." Bhima was contrite. But he saw that Rattan had got over his anger now that he had seen Sunny was not seriously harmed. Turning around so that he was facing Rattan, he said belligerently, "What would you have me do? Did you see the way he was pulling at my arm? The crazy fellow. 'I want to come with you, I want to come with you'," mimicked Bhima shaking his head sideways just like Sunny. Bhima's mimicking Sunny made Rattan laugh softly into the darkness around them. It had been funny, come to think of it.

Sunny pulling Bhima's arm and behaving like a small child. Bhima was immediately assured. There were no hard feelings then, and he was forgiven. That was one of the good things about working with Rattan. You knew exactly what his moods would be. So to make most of the situation now, he continued talking.

"Thanks to Sunny *bhai,*" Bhima said. "He wanted to switch on the lights, to help us pack," he added.

"He wanted to take the TV set too," joined in Rattan, now with good humor restored. All in all it had been a good clean job and profitable at that.

The radio cassette player and the cassettes that Sunny had kindly picked up for them, were left lying outside the gate. "That will puzzle the police no end," was Bhima's comment. The doll would mystify them further. He imagined the police trying to figure out who would want to steal a doll and then leave it lying outside. Visualizing the scene with perplexed police scratching their heads with the doll wildly swaying its hips made Rattan feel good. It was a scene, which made you laugh. He was proud of himself.

CHAPTER IX

What Rattan and Bhima did not know was that Sunny had no way of getting home. The address he had been taught was just so many words to him. Where exactly it was located was beyond him. Nor could he have told anyone, even if there had been someone on that dark and lonely road to guide him that night. Sunny was not going anywhere where he could find himself some help. He passed a traffic cop who tried to stop him but succeeded instead in frightening him so much that Sunny ran blindly, down one road and then another, past houses which were dark and silent or had lights in the windows and sounds of the TV going on inside. The trees bordering the road took on strange menacing forms. They reminded him of the pictures he had seen somewhere. There were no people on the road. Where was everybody?

But soon he came to a crowded market place. People were out even though it was quite late in the night now and some of the small shops were still doing business. Mostly *paan* shops. Bright lights and a crowd of people attracted his attention. Everyone seemed to be rushing in one direction and Sunny followed them. In spite of the pain he was intrigued.

"It is a wedding" was his first excited thought. He could eat now. Visions of hot *chole bhature* flashed into his mind. Yes he decided firmly, he would certainly like one now. Then it struck him that if it was a wedding he could dance. This was something he could do and do well. People clapped and smiled at him whenever he danced. Then his mother or *Bhaiya* would come and take him home.

But following the crowd had brought Sunny to a place, which mesmerized him so much that he stood still. All thoughts of home left him as he stared and drank in the noise and the bustle which went on around him, unmindful of being pushed and jostled around and being cursed for a fool. The tears on his face dried leaving dirt marks. He even stopped feeling hungry. He had no thoughts now of his friends or even wondered where they had gone and why they had left him alone. For he had come to that most magical of all places. He had come to the New Delhi Railway Station.

Sunny followed people going into the railway station with a growing sense of excitement. He was smiling broadly. Chance brought him to the gate when the ticket collector had his back turned. It would have made no difference to Sunny even if he had known that one needed to buy a ticket to get on to a train. Nor did he have the money for it. Again it was chance that pushed him into the line of people getting into a second class compartment. He was transfixed with the sights and the sounds around him. He joined the struggling mass of people at the door of the compartment with a sense of elation. He needed no one to tell him to get into the train. Some of the people did look at him wondering why he was smiling so broadly and at whom he was smiling. As always, his smile indicated much: contentment, acceptance, and above all a happy bravado. A crowd stood outside, peering into windows to recognize friends or relatives who had got in. There was much pushing and shouting since the Jullundur Express was ready to start. People needed to find their berths, settle down, look around and take stock of fellow travelers. This was an important ritual all train travelers went through, most doing it consciously. Sunny merged easily with the mass of people and went along with them being pushed and cursed and stepped into the compartment.

The second class bogie was packed to capacity. Sunny found himself a place between an old lady with a huge basket on her lap and a young man who was already gently snoring, his head thrown back and mouth open. The Delhi-Jullundur Express let out a long and prolonged hoot to tell everyone that it was ready to roll. The engine's hoot made him laugh loudly in sheer delight. This woke up the young man, who looked at him strangely. The old lady smiled kindly at him. She did have a moment's doubt about this strange looking boy but then he was dressed smartly in a pair of fashionable jeans and a sweater. His folks may be in the next compartment. It was such a mad rush on these trains nowadays.

When the train started moving, people relaxed, genial adjustments were made and everyone found a place to sleep. When Sunny got on to the floor between the two berths and stretched himself out, there was general approval. This meant more places for others. Strangely, no one thought of asking him anything, although there was an air of camaraderie in the compartment. People did look at him but made no comments and asked no questions. Finally sleep claimed the travelers one by one and soon there was peace. Sunny stayed awake just long enough to hear the train whistle, sounding lonely and sad as it rushed through the night, its bright lights making a swathe of light before it. Gradually, helped by the motion of the train, he rolled under the seat. He slept there, curled up against the cold and lost among the suitcases and bundles under the seat. He was oblivious to everything. The day's events had been much too much, and sleep came easily and fast casting a kindly pall over him.

This is where the cleaners found him the next morning. They were thorough in their cleaning up since often they found many items careless passengers left behind. Never in all the time they had being working on the trains had they come across someone actually sleeping under the seat. One of them did recall finding a corpse once but even he was not under the seat. The compartment had become empty and how Sunny had missed being spotted earlier was unexplainable. Another mystery was how he could have possibly slept when there was hardly any place for the suitcases and bundles that were pushed under the seats.

Sunny opened his eyes to see a ring of faces looking down on him. A group of men, all in red shirts crowded around him. Some boys who were about his age, jumped on to the seat to get a better look. Rough and callused hands picked him up and deft fingers made sure that there was nothing in his pockets. He seemed to have suffered no serious damage. Unsure how to react to this situation, Sunny did what he always did when he wanted no part of something.

He stood up and without a word walked to the door of the compartment and got off. The surprised *coolies* let him go. On the platform he stood for some time looking around him in bewilderment. Where was he and how did he get here? He looked back at the train in which he had traveled and started to get back into the train. It seemed a safer place than the platform. But the men around him made him sit on one of the benches on the platform. They laughed at him and crowded around him asking him questions. He did not understand what they were saying and this made him sullen. He had no idea what was happening. Why was everyone staring at him? He realized that he was in a new place and there was nothing here, which was familiar. He traveled about 800 miles away from his parents and home but did not know this. So he just sat, feeling a vague sense of fear. He did look around for Rattan or Bhima but could not find them nor could he see anyone he knew. However this situation did not frighten him and like he had done many times before in different places, he waited. Patiently waiting for whatever was to happen to him because he had no control on situations himself, was something he had learnt to do very well.

Groups of *coolies* crowding around some exciting event was not new to Chote Ram, the Station Master. By the way the men bunched around and their stance, he could tell that they were engrossed in something which seemed to hold their attention. Chote Ram was intrigued. Walking over he saw that the center of attraction was a strange looking boy who seemed to be dumb. A chorus of explanations greeted him.

"*Saab*. We found him in the compartment."

"*Saab*. This boy does not speak."

"He does not know anything. What do we do with him?"

"He has no ticket."

"Look in his pockets. Maybe he has lost it."

He looked at the group around him with a half smile. He knew that even if the boy had had something on his person it would have disappeared by now.

"So" he said with an exasperated shake of his head. "What did he have in his pockets? Which one of you took it?"

There was vociferous denial now. *"Nahi Saab."* Why should we *Saab."* "Look at the boy *Saab*. Does he look as if he had anything of value on him?"

Chote Ram had to agree. The boy did have a funny look about him and asking the *coolies* would do no good anyway. He took hold of the boy by his arm and pushed him along into his small cabin. This was not his job. No ticket. The rules were clear. Hand him over to the Railway Police. If, as sometimes happened, the passenger was willing, there were other ways to rectify such... ah, negligence. But this boy seemed to be genuinely puzzled. He did not seem to know what he had done. He had nothing of value on him.

"What do I do now?" he said to himself. Reaching his cabin with half the crowd of *coolies* following him, Chote Ram sat in his chair and looked at the strange looking boy. He stood there, bedraggled and dirty and even though he looked as if he would burst into tears any minute, now he had a dignity about him. He seemed to belong to a respectable family, judging by the clothes he wore.

Chote Ram began the questioning, unmindful of the heads peeking in at the door.

He said sternly "Do you have a ticket?" Silence and a bewildered look.

"Where did you get on to the train?"

Silence.

"Where is your home?" This time there was a quick reply. "Delhi" said Sunny definitely. Then added, "Bhima and Rattan said they would take me to the temple."

"Oh. Where are they - Bhima and Rattan?" asked a relieved Chote Ram. "Did they come with you?"

"They are my friends. I went to their house."

Chote Ram was getting nowhere with this conversation. He tried once more. "Did you tell your parents? Do they know you are in Jullundur?"

Sunny was confused. Did his parents know? He thought they might. He knew he had been with Rattan and Bhima in the night and then he had come to the station instead of going to the temple but perhaps Rattan will come and pick him up from here. He brightened immediately.

"Rattan said he is my friend and he will come," he said.

Chote Ram swore. Of all the things that could happen, he had to be saddled with this boy. He did not want a case of kidnapping or theft or whatever this boy had been doing. He had no time for this. Besides, look at him. This boy did not even know what he was being asked. "We have caught ourselves a *budhu*," he thought and took an instant decision.

"Let him go" he told his assistant. "We don't want the police here and all the problems that will cause. This boy seems to be a *budhu* anyway." So Sunny walked out on to the platform once again. Drawn to a train standing on the lines he walked up to it and stood watching in fascination. No one on that platform in Jullundur Station had really expected him to stay on in the station. Everyone had long gone about his or her respective jobs. After the momentary excitement he had caused on being discovered ticketless, Sunny was forgotten.

Finding himself alone now, Sunny went and sat on the bench he had occupied when they took him off the train. He felt happy sitting on this bench as if it belonged to him. He looked with wonder and mounting interest at the life which went on around him on the platform. He was quite content to be a part of this new life. Sitting on the bench on platform No.2 in Jullundur station, he watched the trains coming in and puffing out. He would perhaps have continued sitting longer if hunger had not made him get up and like a foraging animal go in search of food.

Chote Ram soon discovered that the boy had not left. He did not want another stray in his station. There were already too many. Homeless, abandoned, destitute. He realized that there was something wrong with this boy and though he now knew that he could speak he would never be like the other normal children his age. How old would he be, he wondered? Sixteen? Seventeen? Who were his parents? Were they even now looking for him?

He called Sunny over into his cabin and took out his *tiffin* carrier. *Chappatis, dal* and *aloo gobi.* "Will you have some?" he asked.

Sunny nodded. Soon he was eating hungrily while Chote Ram watched him. He was surprised at himself for the wholly uncharacteristic gesture he had just made. Calling this strange boy in and offering to share his lunch! His mouth twisted in a whimsical smile. There was something in this boy which made you want to reach out to him. He could not understand himself. His wife would never believe him.

51

EPISODE TWO: JULLUNDUR

CHAPTER I

It was well over midnight when Kamal and Pradeep decided that Sunny would not come home that night. Then began the worst time that either Kamal or Prem had experienced. Ringing up friends and asking them whether Sunny had visited them that day. "Is he perhaps with you now, at this very moment." "I am so sorry to wake you up in the middle of the night like this, but have you seen Sunny?" A dialogue that went around in Kamal's head like one of those old fashioned records with a needle stuck in one groove. Relatives had to be asked as well. But, no. No one had seen Sunny. So, that meant only one thing. He was lost and could not find his way home. Delhi was a big city and it could happen to anyone.

Prem had also come to the same conclusion. He had decided to go to the police station and lodge a complaint first thing in the morning. He was not inclined to go immediately to the police. Who knew what Sunny would do? He might just walk in casually not realizing that it was past midnight. Little did they know that the ordeal that started on this night would stretch into long days and nights for many months and the presence of Sunny, his voice, his smile, his laughter would gradually recede into pale memories? Only in Kamal's heart would it be kept alive.

The next morning, November 25th 1992, Kamal and Prem decided to go to the local police station. It was 9.30 a.m. and at this time Sunny was sitting quietly on the bench in Jullundur Railway station while Prem and Kamal sat facing Police Superintendent Vedanayagam in New Delhi. The Greater Kailash Police Station was considered to be one of the best. It was spotlessly clean, which Kamal noted in appreciation. Potted palms lined the corridors. It was crowded and busy. It seemed as if all the people in Delhi were there this morning. Everyone had problems.

They sat close together like two little children thought Constable Daya Ram who was on duty. There was something about them which made people look at them twice. They sat quietly without talking but patiently waiting to be called. One wondered what misfortune had befallen them that they sat so, composed enough, but with a sick fear ready to spring out and which one could see was being kept under control with a great effort.

Behind Kamal was a large chart showing the crimes committed in the city that day. The Station House Officer (SHO) of the Kailash Police Station, Vedanayagam took pride in keeping an up to date record of what was going on in the area under his jurisdiction. It was mandatory police procedure but Vedanayagam took more than ordinary care to chalk up the details. Kamal wondered in passing, "Why chalk and blackboard?" but realized soon enough that given the fast rate at which the figures kept changing this was probably the best way of keeping track and new figures were coming in all the time.

It was an eye opener. The figures were appalling and told their own story. It was easy to see why the police were such a hard pressed lot and perhaps also why many of the crimes went undetected. The chart showed what was happening and had happened just at the beginning of that day and the figures were for just one area. In a sad and frightening testimony to the crime which was a part and parcel of life in Delhi it proclaimed:

Killings 5
Stabbings 12
Kidnapping 8
Bride burning 12
Burglary 11

Kamal was aghast!

One item which had caught and retained her interest was the number chalked against NS. What is NS she had wanted to know. Daya Ram, for that was his name, had been more than eager to explain. NS was the Night Shelter which had been set up by the government but it was they, the police who looked after it.

"Madam ji" he had said, rolling his eyes up heavenwards, "if you go there you will not be able to sleep for a week. It is the place where the homeless and the destitute are taken if they do not have anyone to claim them or no home to go to." With an attempt to paint a more vivid picture for this lady who seemed interested, he said, "It is a scene like you would see in a horror film" he said gaily. Daya Ram was enjoying himself now for he had personally accompanied SHO Vedanayagam to one of the night shelters and was always ready to talk about this experience. He did not notice that the lady seemed suddenly close to tears.

Kamal was indeed stricken. Visions of Sunny in this horror film kept popping up in her mind. Sunny sleeping on the floor shivering with no covering. Sunny made to join a group of drunks and being forced to drink. She saw him fall senseless to the ground, unable to hold the liquor that had been fed to him. But logic prevailed. Who in that night shelter would have enough liquor to give Sunny and more important who would want to part with it? She shook her head as if to clear it of unwelcome thoughts and smiled in relief, recognizing that it was her overactive imagination at work. Again. Frightening though it was, it also gave her a new surge of hope. Perhaps Sunny was in some night shelter. She would go there and see for herself. Vik would take her there. She had not the faintest idea where these shelters were located. So she had a task ahead of her.

But oblivious to the effect he had had on the lady, Daya Ram the police constable was noting down complaints. The lady constable next to him freshened her make-up delicately and kept an amused ear and eye open to the goings on at the next table. The paperwork was done at a really fast clip. Daya Ram had his own way of dealing with people. His comments and one-sided dialogue usually kept the others in the room in splits.

"Servant disappeared with jewelry? Have you written them down in the report? No. No. No. Madam, please itemize them. Gold? Diamonds? Describe them Madam. How do you expect us to help you if you do not give us the details?"

"Madam. Please do not cry. If it is God's will you will get everything back."

"OK. Next."

"Uncle not giving back money borrowed many years ago. Given in good faith. But Sir, did you even think twice before lending your hard earned money."

"What will the police do now eh? Run after this man? This is not a police case, Sir. Go to a lawyer first. What is the world coming to these days? You can't trust your own kith and kin."

"Woman beaten black and blue by the husband. *Toba. Toba.* Madam. You will have to show us the evidence."

"No. Madam. We have ladies for this job. Please wait madam. Next."

"Another case of servant disappearing? Why do the public not register the servants when they are appointed?" This addressed to the air above his head and the mock sorrow on his face drove home the point to the couple in front of him.

When it was Prem and Kamal's turn Daya Ram took the forms they had filled in with laborious meticulousness. A missing son? Even Daya Ram could understand the agony of this. He was as gentle as time and a long waiting line of people would allow. When the lady insisted on seeing the SHO personally Daya Ram shrugged his shoulders and rolled his eyes up expressively. Everyone wanted to see the SHO. Why? When he was here specifically to do their bidding? A servant of the people. He addressed the room generally. But the elderly couple stood silently in front of him a little embarrassed but by no means intimidated. They understood and even sympathized with him. Seeing that his persuasive powers were ineffective, Daya Ram got up from his chair reluctantly with the air of one doing a great favor.

"Well, if you have the time to wait by all means do so," he said, implying that he had things to do and he could not sit and wait like them. But as it happened SHO Vedanayagam rang his buzzer just then wanting to know if there were any people waiting to see him before he went away on his round of inspection. Daya Ram well knew that his superior's often repeated dictum was "Treat all elderly people like your parents." He acted with alacrity. "I will make a special request to my superior to see you," he told them. Ushering in this couple now Daya Ram expected his SHO to tell him, his deputy to see to their comfort. He had already done so and had even given them chairs to sit on. Daya Ram felt the virtuous glow of someone who has done a good job without being told.

SHO Vedanayagam fancied himself as a counselor. He often told his subordinates that if they only listened to the people who came to the police station for help carefully, they would soon learn to untangle the problems. According to him, everything boiled down to wrongly handled relationships and an inability to 'adjust' to situations and to people. This was his favorite word, 'adjust'. Certainly the people who came to him could almost always benefit more from counseling than actual police work. He would shrug eloquently and say with a half smile "But I am a policeman. Not a counselor. Though I play the role of one whenever I have the chance."

When Kamal and Prem came into his room, his policeman instinct told him that here was a couple with what he called a 'genuine' story. They were here to report their missing son. He had disappeared the night before and had not returned. Vedanayagam's mind meticulously ticked off all the possibilities.

Murder? Kidnap? Maybe even a little affair on the side without his parents knowing? Drugs? A runaway? Anything could have happened to their son. Delhi was a big city and the numerous activities of the underworld were mind boggling. He knew that the man and woman who now sat patiently would recoil in horror if he even suggested what might have happened to their son. He did not want to increase their apprehension. He was cordial and listened with admirable patience to the story they told him. He ignored Daya Ram's head, which appeared every now and then from behind the screen that partitioned his room from the area set aside for meetings with his subordinates. He had the effusive hospitality of the true southerner. Although it was not his home he treated his office as if it were an extension of his home. To do the SHO credit, he had gauged at one glance that it was more than just a missing son. He was intrigued. This elderly husband and wife seemed agonized and were truly troubled.

Kamal started to talk and Prem sat loyally by her side. It was a sad story of love made impossible by the boy's disability. If the boy was intellectually disabled, there was little chance of his ever being found. He wondered whether they had already sent out a search party. No. They said. They had not done anything as yet. They had come straight to the police. Daya Ram standing behind the screen shook his head in mock despair. Such touching faith in the police! In spite of his interest and in spite of wanting to help them Vedanayagam could not really do anything for them He was at pains to make them realize that as the police they would indeed do everything in their power to find the boy.

"But one has to be realistic madam," he said, shaking his head. "Delhi is a very big city." He added again with emphasis "Very, very big."

Seeing the look of hopelessness on the faces of the two sitting in front of him, he hastened to add "Of course we will do our best." He called Daya Ram to his side and said in clearly articulated words, so that the old couple would hear and be impressed.

"Daya Ram, give them form number MS149. Make very sure that you get all the details correctly. You understand? Absolutely no gray areas."

"This is for reporting missing persons he told them. We will alert the Missing Persons Squad. They will visit all the places he used to frequent and see if anyone had heard or seen anything."

"And put it on the TV?" suggested Daya Ram. The SHO nodded his head in agreement. "Certainly," he said. "Try the TV also. Sometimes it did bring in results in the most amazing way." He nodded to Daya Ram as he stood up.

"Constable Daya Ram will look after you," he said and with a glance at Daya Ram, which spoke volumes, he strode out of the room. Long suffering Daya Ram understood the look. It said, "Give this couple your complete attention. Make them go away happy. Be nice to them."

Daya Ram had no problems with this. Here was another couple, another case, and the SHO wanted more than ordinary courtesies shown to them for some reason. If that is what the SHO wanted, I suppose that is what I will do thought Daya Ram. What he would never ever guess was that at the sight of Kamal, SHO Vedanayagam's thoughts had flown all the way to his little village in Kuppam, where his mother still lived in happy solitude. Her one great blessing was the son who was a big police officer in Delhi. Thoughts of paddy fields under a blazing sun and green coconut palms swaying in the breeze went with SHO Vedanayagam in his chauffeur driven police car.

Back with Daya Ram, Kamal wrote down details of Sunny. What was he wearing when he left home?

Blue jeans and a striped sweater. Red and green.

How old was he?

Almost twenty.

Any distinguishing marks? Birthmarks?

No. But he did have the look of all children with Downs Syndrome.

Downs Syndrome? What is that??

"Oh. My God!" exclaimed Daya Ram involuntarily when Sunny's disability was explained to him. This piece of information stumped him for a time. How on earth could one trace someone who did not even know his address and would most probably be unable to relate the circumstances of his disappearance? If ever he was found, thought Daya Ram. The more details he heard about this boy called Sunny, the more he despaired. A boy like that could be anywhere. With anyone. Who was to know? He could even be dead.

Finally with all the details written down in triplicate, Kamal and Prem were free to leave. Kamal felt a faint surge of hope. Maybe the police could locate Sunny. After all he could not have gone very far. How could he, when he had no money and no knowledge of the geography of Delhi. It was a better frame of mind than Prem's who sat silent and grim throughout. In a complete reversal of his optimism the night before, he was now fully convinced that Sunny was in serious trouble. He refused to allow himself to harbor even an iota of faith in the police. Besides he had talked to Naidu and seen his face blanche when he mentioned Sunny. Something had very definitely happened to Sunny. But what and where, was something, which defied the imagination.

So it was a silent and apprehensive couple that returned home that day. Ajay was waiting for news. No, they had no news to give. Ajay himself had been out half the night roaring on his motorbike up and down the by lanes of the area near the house in search of Sunny. He was all set to continue his search again. Like his father he had little faith in what the police could do. Not that he dismissed the reach the police had but he knew better than most that his brother's intellectual disability would pose problems for anyone who really seriously wanted to help him. He also knew of Sunny's innate desire for adventure and the ease with which he could make himself comfortable in any situation. A more alarming thought was the ease with which Sunny could endear himself to people. It did not take much for people to respond positively to Sunny. His innocent charm and his spontaneous laughter were infectious and caught people unawares. It was a rare characteristic in a world where everyone and everything was suspect. Invariably, people found themselves going out of their way to do things for him. So, where Sunny was and what he was doing was something best left to God, felt Ajay. But he was sure about one thing. Wherever he was, Sunny would survive. If he was alive. A sobering and chilling thought which he did not share with his mother.

CHAPTER II

As Sunny grew, both Kamal and Prem had learnt to live with a son who would never fulfill the dreams they had for him. They had learnt what disability and specifically intellectual disability was all about. Kamal had learnt to introduce Sunny to friends and relatives who came to visit. "My son," she would say and wait for the quick exchange of glances between the couple. Sunny did look different. His eyes slanted as if he had oriental blood in him and he had blunt features and stubby fingers.

People would often react with unusually loud and bright "Hellos." Kamal would react with a bright smile. "He is not deaf as well," she would say and laugh to show that it was alright for them to make such a mistake. Even relatives would take furtive looks at her and Prem as if they had done something they could not understand. None of this escaped her and she noted everything with a defiant determination as if to say whatever you think or feel, this is my son. I love him.

In time they had learnt to adjust. It was Sunny himself who had helped with this. Unfailingly cheerful, he kept them all amused with the things he did and said. As he grew into an adolescent, people who knew him became genuinely fond of him. He had a busy life. Kamal enrolled him in the school for children like Sunny in Okhla. He liked getting dressed and going off to school like everyone else. Waiting for the bus to come, often with his mother or father keeping him company was a special time. He did comprehend how good it was to have his parents waiting with him. It gave him a sense of security. The bus picked him up at 8.00 a.m. sharp. Sunny greeted his friends at each stop with genuine enthusiasm. He enjoyed the stops the bus made on its way to school and it somehow made this ordinary journey into one full of excitement and possibilities. Some of the other children caught his enthusiasm and if Sunny was absent the whole bus would be silent until school was reached. These morning rides were a joy. He liked meeting his friends, the driver of the bus and the conductor. His main concern was whether his mother had given him the *tiffin* he wanted to take. It became a family joke. Sunny and his *tiffin*. His happiness was infectious. His laughter, often at the silliest of things, and above all his penchant for making friends made him very popular in school. His greatest need and his greatest gift was making friends. He would go anywhere he was welcomed and treated with some kindness.

The years had passed so swiftly and before they knew it, he had grown to be a young man with a young man's body and feelings. It was the innocent charm of a small child, which spoke the truth about Sunny and his disability. The special school he attended could not provide him with the kind of activities and excitement he craved. Kamal understood his need for company, for friends to hang out with, for girl friends and for the sheer freedom of being able to do whatever he wanted. Her heart ached for him. So, when he returned from school she would often encourage him to go out to meet his friends. She knew that the market round the corner was one of his favorite places. In fact everyone in the neighborhood knew his routine. If he was not in the market at his usual time, people missed him.

But sometimes Sunny would suddenly decide not to go to the market or anywhere for that matter. What brought on this change in routine was something he did not know. It just happened. But on these days you could see him parading up and down the terrace of his home with a stick in his hand from which fluttered a piece of green cloth. Not many people knew that to Sunny the terrace was the railway station and that he was the Station Master. He was the one responsible for all the trains coming in and going out. It was all a glorious mix of noise and excitement, which he alone could see. After watching him with some perplexity on several occasions Kamal had one day suddenly realized why there was such a fascination for the terrace. The obsession with trains had begun when they had taken him to the station to meet his aunt. No one guessed at the tremendous impact this visit had on Sunny. To him it was magical. The huge trains with their smoke and noise, puffing into the station like some medieval dragon, caused the same kind of excitement in Sunny that a real dragon would have caused to a normal child had some magic made it appear in the middle of the city.

Kamal had not realized that Sunny had been so observant or that he had managed to take in so much of what he had seen in the station. It was only after he kept parading on the terrace and kept asking her for a flag that she had known what an impact his first visit to the station had been. After that, either Prem or his brother Ajay would take him to the station whenever they needed to go to receive or see someone off. This was a rare treat for which Sunny would do anything. Kamal often wondered whether he could actually visualize the trains. What went on in his head when he waved his green flag so enthusiastically? She would never know. Whatever it was that Sunny saw in his mind's eye, which kept him, so occupied was something beyond his capacity for communication.

Sunny doing his station master role became a familiar sight to the neighbors and they would good naturedly go along with his fantasy. Kamal and Prem also became used to this. When he was not away in the market or the temple he was bound to be on the terrace.

They gradually learnt to know what his limitations were. The counselor in the special school he attended had told them that he would never be able to read or write. They knew that he would never be able to be on his own. He was happy when they gave him his food or brought him a small token of their affection. His wants were few and his capacity to melt into any situation as if he belonged was immense.

CHAPTER III

As days passed into weeks and then into months Kamal hit peaks of hope and depths of despair. She kept the memories of Sunny alive by deliberately thinking about him. Two incidents took pride of place in Kamal's memories of Sunny. Thinking about it now Kamal had to hastily wipe the tears from her eyes. If Prem saw her he would surely break down. How well she knew him. Here they both sat as if it was like any other day. The waiting for Sunny tucked away uneasily somewhere in the backs of their minds, although it was now six months since he had disappeared and everyone had given up hope that they would ever see him again. But to Kamal and Prem, the hope that some day Sunny would come home was always a possibility, and alive. But that day had not come. The fears they had both hidden so well had gradually surfaced and forced them to look at the harsh reality. They learnt to face the fact that in a violent and uncaring world Sunny on his own may not survive. It was an unspoken acceptance. Neither of them voiced it to the other but in the unspoken way couples can communicate, each knew that the other had accepted this reality. There was really no need to talk about it at all.

Kamal could switch herself on and off when her thoughts went to Sunny, but even as she fed on her memories, she was conscious of a parallel stream of thought, like a monologue going on inside her head that said things like, "Will Sunny survive out there? Will he be able to look after himself? But he was like a child… Will he be able to get some food to eat? Is he starving? Is he cold?" And so this went on, often accompanied by fearsome scenes of Sunny in all sorts of situations. How adept she had become over the months. How had she ever survived this period of waiting for Sunny? Even Prem could only dimly feel her pain and her grief. It was like having him die but worse because she knew that when he left home he was a happy, alive person and visualizing him dead was impossible.

But sometimes she would escape into the happy memories of Sunny. It made her feel as if nothing drastic had really happened. She loved to think back at all the silly things he had said and done. She smiled to herself as she thought about the day when Prem had brought home a new music system for Ajay. Sunny had walked into the drawing room and had stood still when he saw it. Ajay was happily fiddling with the system and he had all his cassettes strewn over the floor. Sunny was enchanted. He knew what Ajay was doing. He had seen similar things in other houses and now there was one in his house. As always he took it for granted that this, like everything in the house belonged to him as well. He had never experienced the concept of single ownership. "I will listen to music every day" he said, the delight obvious on his face. It was a statement made to assure himself of future musical delights rather than a question. Sunny was used to getting most of the things he asked for. So he fully expected that the music system too would be his.

Kamal remembered how long she had taken to explain the situation to him.

"No. Sunny. This is *Bhaiya's*. You must ask him if you want to play it."

Sunny was bewildered. "A music system like this one is very expensive," she had explained. "It is not like buying toffees or a coke." They did not have enough money to buy two. "But he could use *Bhaiya's* if he was careful." Unfortunately it was not so easily solved. Ajay was rightly apprehensive about his new equipment. He had a treasured collection of cassettes, which he kept in a special box he had made. One could understand why he just would not allow Sunny to play his cherished cassettes unless he was with him in the room and then too under his supervision. This was not what Sunny wanted. Whenever he wanted the music turned on which was often, but not allowed to do so, he would invariably end up shouting in anger or sobbing in frustration.

But things did settle down gradually and Sunny stopped asking for the music to be put on. It did not come as a surprise to Kamal when she discovered that Sunny had watched Ajay and had learnt how to use the system. Even now Kamal wondered how he had learnt the art of dissembling. He was careful not to play it when Ajay was at home but when either his father or mother were around he knew that all they would say was "be careful with *Bhaiya's* things". In fact, Kamal admitted to herself now, he was really careful with the equipment, putting away all the music cassettes he had used and wiping them lovingly with a cloth. He even covered it up with the green and yellow dust cover she had made. Ajay, when he did come to know of Sunny's using the equipment behind his back, had to agree that somehow he had taught himself how to use it. So finally he had agreed to allow Sunny to play all the music he wanted, provided that he put everything away. So the problem of the music system was solved peacefully.

But it led to a very interesting development. Kamal laughed softly as she saw in her mind's eye Sunny's accurate impersonations of the dancers he saw on the TV. He could do it all. He could shake his hips and make the pelvic thrusts and weird head actions, which passed for dance in the Hindi films. She had been so very delighted at his achievement. Particularly since he had taught himself. His only teachers were the stars of the Hindi film which the whole family would watch every Sunday. It was a special treat for Sunny when they borrowed a film from the video shop round the corner and it was sure to get Sunny's approval if it had dance sequences. He was so good, keeping the rhythm and the beat as if born to it.

What could he not have done had he not been born with Downs Syndrome was something about which she had often fantasized.

CHAPTER IV

Over the months that followed Sunny's disappearance, Kamal kept herself busy trying to get some information about night shelters. Constable Daya Ram had suggested she could check them out if she wished. He had been most helpful in getting her addresses and details of their location. She knew of the existence of five night shelters in the city of Delhi. She was amazed. Never had she dreamt that so many people needed such a facility or that the city fathers in their wisdom had actually provided it. Out of the five, three were in old Delhi. After some thought Kamal decided to begin with the two which were comparatively closer to her home. Even these were too far away for Sunny to have reached there, but who could say what had actually happened. He may have been taken there or God forbid the thought, somehow lured away to join the homeless wanderers who begged their way through life.

This was Kamal's secret and most haunting fear. Neither Prem nor Ajay knew that she thought endlessly about this possibility. Kamal would see herself driving through crowded traffic and suddenly she would spot Sunny, with palm outstretched in the universal and eternal gesture of want. She would scream out his name. "Sunny. Sunny *beta*." But always in her dreams, Sunny would look at her unseeingly without a flicker of recognition in his eyes and then walk away. Soon he would be lost in the crowds. Kamal would wake up shivering and miserable. But she never once shared this devastating fear with anyone else. It was her own private agony.

So, it was almost five to six months before she steeled herself to actually visit one of the night shelters in Delhi. The Night Shelter in Khale Khan turned out to be what she had expected. A long low building with windows every two feet but barred with thick steel rods. A door with steel bars painted a rusty red completing the illusion that the people inside were prisoners, waiting for whatever was their destiny. The smell of phenyl and urine was overpowering.

Kamal covered her nose and mouth with the end of her saree. It was a place that would depress the most stoic she felt. Even though she had come in the morning, when most of its occupants had gone away on their daily businesses, wisely deciding that seeing it at night may neither be safe nor allow her peace of mind, there were some who stayed simply because they had nowhere to go and nothing to do. Two men cowered in the corner. One was obviously very ill and was being tended by the other younger man. Kamal averted her face but not before she had seen the haggard face of the man on the floor. Maybe he is dying she thought and irrationally began to think about how and why he could have arrived at such a destination. The younger one seemed plainly resigned to his situation and even managed a grin as she passed him and made a half salute to her. Kamal looked again at the man with surprise but decided that the salute was for the man in charge who stood at the door keeping an eye on her. But Sunny, to her great relief was not there. Neither did questioning the two occupants indicate that anyone even remotely resembling Sunny had been there. Not for the past two months at least.

Back home Kamal washed herself several times before she felt she had sloughed away the smell and the desperation she seemed to have imbibed from the night shelter she had visited. She reasoned that Sunny would have made some attempts to come home or talked to people. The thought that he could have somehow gone out of Delhi was too frightening to even think about.

CHAPTER V

Soon after the music system episode an amused neighbor rushed in one evening and pulled Kamal out of the house.

"You must see this," he said. "You must."

On the street outside the gate a wedding procession had stopped. The *baraat* had yet to come and the wedding guests and family of the bride were passing the time by dancing to the music provided by the hired music band. SHIV MOHAN BAND read the legend on the banner in letters of red and gold. Two members of the band, looking important and dressed in special tunics of blue velvet carried the banner, while the musicians looked resplendent in their white uniforms with the same red and gold letters of the banner on a band around their arm. The music they provided had its own charm. Familiar pop songs were taken and so twisted out of their original music through brass suddenly taking off on a highly individual note and percussion that drowned every other instrument, that it turned the song being played into a strange new incarnation but yet so very familiar.

But it was not the music or the musicians that had started the crowd swaying and clapping. But the twirling figure of Sunny right in the middle of the crowd, dancing with abandon and a precision which was a joy to see. The applause of the crowd only egged him on to try new improvisations in steps and movements. He ended up doing an absolutely fantastic performance, little realizing that he was entertaining a crowd of some hundred people all on his own.

If Sunny's new found expertise in dance amazed and delighted, it was not so with his sudden fascination with cars. His pleadings to be allowed to drive the family 1990 Fiat strained Kamal's patience to the limit. Kamal did realize that as a teenager it was an expected interest. Others may have collected pictures of cars and certainly there would have been much pouring over magazines which carried glossy pictures. For Sunny it was just the great need to sit behind the wheel of the car and zoom around Delhi. He wanted desperately to be seen by everyone, actually driving a car. Kamal wondered whether he actually saw himself waving to his friends and incredulous passers by. Did he also hear people cheer as he whizzed by saying "there goes Sunny in his CAR." There was no way of knowing what he thought because what he said was far removed from what he wanted to say.

Kamal understood him and also knew that it did not occur to Sunny that driving a car was not an easy thing. He could not understand why his father and brother could drive it but not him. His delight in just getting into the car and being taken for a ride was touching. How many times had she made use of this to bring him out of bad moods, his tantrums and stubborn refusal to do what was required of him and even his rare moments of sadness.

Prem was sure that they could not prevent Sunny from trying his hand at driving the car. It could happen any time. So, he had hidden the keys of the car, changing its place from time to time and quite often confusing himself in the process when he could not remember where the last hiding place was. It had not really helped though because Sunny would burst into tears when he was refused the keys to the car. Patient explanations, promises and a sigh of relief when he finally decided that he would not drive that day was an event that happened periodically. Sunny never gave up trying his luck over and over again. "He is like a bulldog' Prem often said in amusement. "Never lets go."

The situation had come to such that thinking of taking the car out became a nightmare. It was Ajay who came to the rescue. He was the one who really understood Sunny, Kamal felt. She knew that he had always felt that but for the grace of God he could have been like Sunny. It made him protective but not emotional the way she often allowed herself to become. Ajay was very aware of the things Sunny was missing and what he could have been doing had he been normal.

He realized that Sunny just wanted to be around the car and did not really mean that he wanted to drive it. The next best thing would be to allow him to tinker with his motorbike.

On a Sunday afternoon, Ajay had taken the time to teach Sunny the finer nuances of motorbike cleaning. This had made Sunny deliriously happy. It was not only that he was allowed to actually touch his brother's motorbike but that it was Ajay who was with him, spending time with him and most glorious of all doing something together. But Ajay, as meticulous about his bike cleaning as he was about his music system made very sure that Sunny would understand the importance of not touching the bike without his permission. The punishment would be instant banishment from the glory of bike cleaning. Only if he was very careful, very good, would he be allowed to clean his bike again. Sunny seemed to understand, because he never once transgressed the limits put on him. Kamal had been amazed at how instinctively Sunny had known that obeying Ajay was something, which he just had to do, while obeying her could be sometimes overlooked.

For Sunny being allowed to clean Ajay's motorbike brought in days of unsullied happiness. He desperately wanted to please his brother. To Sunny, Ajay was the kind of person he wanted to be. Kamal shook her head ruefully. Yes, Sunny wanted to ride a bike, go out with friends to a movie, sit around in his room with a couple of his friends and talk endlessly. He wanted to go to the shops and select the music he liked and then come home and play the cassette. She knew what bliss this would have meant for him. Sunny had known that he could never do all that Ajay did. It was an acceptance of himself as he was with no ambitions, not striving to go beyond his capacity and absolutely no envy of his brother. God had loaded one side of the balance with the gift of unsullied happiness while weighing down the other with difficulties caused by his disability. "God, please be with him," whispered Kamal now, softly to herself. She felt that if she persisted in her prayers and kept asking God over and over again, he would indeed answer her prayers.

CHAPTER VI

Chote Ram often wondered about Sunny. Who was he? Where had he come from? He was also beginning to get very fond of this boy, *budhu* though he was. He smiled as he thought of the many things which Sunny did and said, which caused much merriment among those who had formed themselves into a protective group around him. This in itself was an amazing thing, that these children, who were themselves fair prey to a host of unpleasant things happening to them, should have felt drawn to look after someone they felt needed help more than they did.

On a cold day in November, six months ago, the *coolies* had unceremoniously bundled Sunny out of the compartment in which he had been sleeping, looking like a bundle of rags and shivering in the cold of that misty morning. It had been the train which had come in from Delhi. The boy had had no ticket. He had not the faintest notion where he was headed. Talking to him had elicited only one bit of information. That his name was Sunny. He either did not remember or could not put what he had to say in intelligible language. However many times he was asked questions about himself, he always came up with the same answers. He had come from Delhi and he had come on the train. He could add nothing new to what he had already told them a hundred times. Soon, everyone realized that Sunny's speech was unclear and it needed the greatest of effort to make out what he was trying to say. It was far easier to just let him be.

The ease with which Sunny had escaped the notice of those who were ever alert for new game made him in Chote Ram's eyes at least, someone very special. The gods protect the innocent, he recalled and this boy with his strange looks and his infectious good cheer seemed truly protected. When all attempts at trying to find his home address or anything about his family had proved useless, Chote Ram had put an advertisement in the local language papers, hoping that someone somewhere would read it and he would at last be able to entrust this boy to someone who knew him. Days went by and then months with not a single reply. Chote Ram gave up hoping. The boy was here to stay and somehow he felt responsible. Just as he did for the other children who strayed on to his platform or were deliberately lost there for reasons only the tortured souls of those who brought them there would know.

Sometimes, a sudden munificence would descend on the children in the form of some rich woman in chiffon and diamonds who would direct her servants to feed fifty children. Her place in Heaven was assured with this. On such occasions which came all too rarely the servants would round up any children they could find. Many of the children saw to it that Sunny was one of those fed that day. He could not or would not make any attempts to clamor for attention like the rest of them did. Although they did not understand this in Sunny, they good naturedly put it down to another aspect of his being different from them.

On these lucky days, men and women would shepherd them into long lines. "*Chalo. Chalo. Bachon.* Sit in a line. You will all get something. Don't push. Don't crowd." It was a treat the children waited for avidly and discussed long after it was over. Someone or the other was always there to see that Sunny did get a fair share of the *puri*s and *bhaji* or the *halwa* which was distributed on very special festival days. Most often this would be Bintu, the boy who helped the *puri wallah* and who had lived on this platform for as long as he could remember. Sunny would eat his fill and if he could have done so, he would have gravely thanked the people responsible for this largesse. Such happenings must have brought up at least vague scenes in his head of other times and other days. What did he really remember of his far off days in Delhi? Nobody knew.

The little urchins who lived on the platform found in Sunny a never ceasing source of amusement. To the older boys he was an object of amused tolerance. These boys, even the tiniest ones, were wise beyond their years. Some of them came in everyday with their parents who worked in the yard or had small eating places on the

73

platform. So, all of them were familiar with the sight of Sunny sitting on the bench he considered his home turf. They looked forward to being greeted by him with his friendly smile and wave of the hand. What however, gave them all real delight was to see Sunny do his Station Master's role. How he had picked it up remained a mystery but Sunny knew with an amazing instinct when each train was due. He would wait for Chote Ram to come and position himself just behind him. Like Chote Ram, Sunny also had managed to get what for him passed as a flag. A stick with a cloth attached to it. Then would follow a ritual which the regulars on the platform had come to expect and even look forward to. Once he located the station master and took up his own position, which would be a place from where he could see Chote Ram he would copy every movement of his arms and legs. Eyes squinting with concentration and legs spread apart just the correct distance, he did indeed look as if many things depended on him. Sunny did see himself as the one in charge of the platform and he performed his duties of waving the trains in and out with great seriousness.

He did not remember very clearly when or how he had come to this platform or to this station in Jullundur. It would have made little difference even if he had known. He felt that it was up to him to keep control over the trains coming in and going out. Without him nothing there would move. Why the trains moved at the mere flick of a flag was beyond him nor was he interested. It was sufficient that they did. He had no doubts at all that it was because of him. Of course the station master also helped. Slowly everything else in his life began to fade away gently into the distance, leaving him with the here and now. His platform. His trains. His new friends. The station was now his life.

The trains were always crowded and every time a train came in or left there was chaos. People who had just come in rushed about trying to locate their respective bogies. Women ran behind their men folk, managing with admirable adroitness to hold on to wailing children and at the same time baskets loaded with food and bulging bags. The *chai wallah* and the *puri wallah* sweated in happy agony as they strained themselves to cater to the demands of their customers. Once this train left, there would be time to settle back and rest. But now it was money making time. Those already in the train looked with impatience at the madness outside. When was the train going to move?

When the trains started rumbling slowly out of the station the sound of the wheels, the shrill whistle it made as it pulled out, and the sight of this huge monster making its way out of the station excited Sunny as nothing else could. When people inside the train smiled at him or waved back as some of them did, Sunny was in his element. The noise and confusion, the yelling people, the mountains of luggage, the *coolies* rushing around trying to fit odd shaped bundles and boxes and bedding of all shapes and sizes into often insufficient space, under seats, overhead, balanced precariously on other boxes, all contributed towards making this a time of pure bliss.

To Chote Ram who was aware of Sunny behind him imitating his actions, this was an assurance that the boy was still on the platform and all was well. He would walk back to his cabin wondering for the hundredth time who this boy was and how he had got here. A railway station platform of all places! He knew that within minutes Sunny would join him and sit silently on the rickety steel chair in the corner.

Sunny coming in to sit with him in his cabin had become a necessity brought about by an alarming development. It had made a nervous wreck of Chote Ram some months ago. The day he would long remember had began with news that Sunny had gone. No one had seen him leave the station. Chote Ram knew as did the others, that Sunny would fall prey to the first unscrupulous man if he had managed to get into the city. He had come amongst them suddenly one day and now, as suddenly he had gone. Chote Ram could not suppress the twinges of anxiety nor control his frequent scanning of the platform as if hoping to see the familiar figure of Sunny sitting on his favorite bench. But the next day, to his relief he was back. Once again, as had happened when he first came to Jullundur, asking him brought only the vaguest of answers, As far as Chote Ram could make out Sunny had been traveling on the Jullundur-Ludhiana train whenever he felt the urge to do so. It was as simple as that. Up and down, up and down. How long he had been doing this and how he had escaped the ticket collectors clutches so far was a mystery. After the first episode it had happened several times. Sunny would not be there one day and reappear the next day as if he had never stepped out of the station. Each time this happened, Chote Ram went through a time of unshakable tension to be replaced by a similar relief once Sunny returned. Everyone now knew that Sunny just stepped into the Ludhiana Express in the night and reaching Ludhiana spent the day on the station there presumably and caught the night train from there back to Jullundur. The ease with which he had understood this was something Chote Ram found difficult to believe. From what he now knew of Sunny and his limited intellectual capacities this precision in timing and travel seemed impossible. Yet Sunny had done the impossible Chote Ram felt he could never fathom this strange boy who had come into his life. Once again, here was proof that some strange power kept Sunny from coming to any serious harm. But enough was enough and finally Chote Ram made it a rule that Sunny should come and sit with him in his cabin once the trains were flagged out. Sunny obeyed without murmur and his escapades stopped. So it was Chote Ram himself who had started this routine of Sunny coming into his cabin and sitting in the chair placed there for him.

Sunny's new life in Jullundur as a member of the platform dwellers slowly began to take shape and meaning. When he had first found himself in an unfamiliar new place, apprehension had made him keep to himself. Now, finding a place to sleep every night like the other boys on the platform and eating whatever was handed out to him by passengers or *coolies* who took pity on him, became his daily routine. Gradually, his life fell into a regular routine where just the need for sheer survival became the most important thing in his life. After the initial excitement of the newness Sunny introduced into the lives of the others who lived on the platform, things settled down in patterned eddies around him. Slowly but irrevocably he changed from a novelty to a regular. Sunny, if he had understood the implications of this, would have been delighted. It meant that he finally belonged. He was part of the platform culture. He could now claim allegiance and expect loyalty from the members of this tight knit group of people who for various reasons and circumstances, found that in the railway station lay their final destiny. Most of all it meant that he would merit the fierce and loyal protection of the group and they would look after him.

The Sunny of Delhi was gradually being shaped into someone who had to learn to face each day as it came. He accepted everything that happened to him whether good or hurting, with an equanimity and lack of criticism that would have been the envy of those longing for exactly this ego-less existence through long hours of meditation. He had vague memories of home and particularly of his mother but only vaguely remembered his life in Delhi.

CHAPTER VII

One day Sunny had made an astounding announcement at dinner. The characteristic shake of his head and lopsided happy smile indicated that he had some momentous news. "I want to marry Gita," he had said with a certainty that would have been amusing if it had not seemed so impossible. He looked at his father and his mother in turn as if now that he had said it, it would happen. Incredulous at first, the rest of them had soon learnt from Sunny that there was indeed a Gita. Ajay who knew her filled in the details. She was a first year student doing her Masters in Social Work. Her family had recently moved into the neighborhood. She had told Ajay that she had often seen Sunny parading up and down on his terrace, doing his Station Master's role and had responded to Sunny's cheery "Hello." Ever willing to make new friends Sunny had become a regular visitor at her home. He would stop just long enough to shout out a greeting and then be on his way hurrying on to some destination which only he knew.

The day had come when like any other teenager Sunny had started showing signs of independence. He would come back from school and promptly go out again to be with his friends. Kamal knew who his friends were. She was not unduly worried since they all knew Sunny. They had sympathized with her when she first told them of Sunny's problems. She would immediately come to know if anything happened to him.

But marry Gita!! This took the situation into realms which she had not as yet thought about. Apparently he knew enough to appreciate femininity and she had not noticed the awakening of his seemingly latent sexuality. How blind she had been!! Gita. Yes, she was very charming. Round faced with a wide dimpled smile she was disarmingly straightforward. Her hair was cut short which gave her a cute pert look. There was no two ways about Gita. It was either a 'Yes' or a 'No'. This was what perhaps endeared her to people. The group of young people she hung out with thought she was someone very special. She had heard Ajay say so often enough. Kamal knew many young men in the colony thought so. Her poor Sunny was not the only one.

When he had started going around to her house he had been just one among the many, both boys and girls who regularly congregated there. Being a student of social science Gita had a special interest in Sunny. Her interest had been more academic, for in college she had heard for the first time about Downs Syndrome and had thenceforth gone out of her way to be extra nice to Sunny. Little dreaming that in so doing she was awakening long dormant and dimly understood stirrings within Sunny.

Although quite disconcerted at this romantic development in Sunny's life and not quite knowing what to do, Kamal had tried to talk gently to Sunny. But she found she did not have the faintest clue how or what to say. She knew that the implications of marriage was beyond his understanding. But she did wonder. Did he understand about love? About sex? Or had he perhaps learnt whatever he knew by watching torrid scenes on the TV? But gradually she realized that Sunny did not have the faintest clue either. Marrying Gita was something he thought he should do. Was it more a desire for companionship? For a friend who asked no questions and did not criticize?

For Sunny, Gita was a source of great delight. He liked being with her and listening to her. Although he had some acquaintance with the other boys who were part of her life he often wished that they would leave her alone. He wanted what everyone who ever fancied a girl wants. To be the only one in her life. He was sure that he liked her very much and if boys and girls liked each other a lot they got married. His conversations with his mother now began to undergo a subtle change. He quoted Gita on everything. He would try his best to put on his red shirt because Gita liked it. Sometimes he would even take it off from the pile of dirty washing where it was kept for the next day's laundry. It was Gita said this and Gita said that. It was amusing and tragic. The reality was that Sunny would never have a Gita of his own.

Torn between the desire to explain about the birds and the bees and wondering where to draw the fine line, Kamal decided to ignore the whole situation. As it happened this seemed to be the right approach. Sunny's oft repeated statement that he wanted to marry Gita gradually gave way to more immediate pastimes. His life went ahead occupied fully with today, with the many interesting things that were happening all around him. All of which were immensely interesting even if he did not understand whatever he was captivated with at the moment.

He did succeed in proving a point though. That he was now a man with the emotions, the sexual feelings and the desire to interact with the opposite sex just like any normal teenager. His brief foray into romantic life had given Kamal and Prem a jolt. In a way Kamal was glad at this display of a normal emotion but also frightened at the dawning realization that pretty soon they may face a real crisis. Sunny's awakening manhood brought with it a host of new problems. It was difficult to see the man Sunny in him though. The boy Sunny with his boisterous laugh and his behavior which was that of a gullible child often intermingled with the serious Sunny who wanted to do adult things. Kamal was never quite sure when man would take over boy.

The episode had some repercussions. Gita, when she came to know of Sunny's announcement at the dinner table was contrite. She blamed herself. So she took extra trouble to talk to him explaining why she could not marry him.

"I have to finish college you see, Sunny. I must get a job."

"OK." from an obedient Sunny.

"You must finish your school also Sunny. It is important."

"OK." From a suddenly serious Sunny since Gita said he had to go to school.

So it was, that what Kamal could not do, Gita did. She directed his energies and his thoughts onto other things. Relieved at the ease with which Sunny had got over Gita (had he really though, wondered Kamal?), Kamal became complacent. When Sunny started going to the temple nearby she was overjoyed. Here at least he will be away from the temptations he faced in the market place which had been his favorite haunt. But one never knew what Sunny would do and where he would go. He did whatever he felt he should do without any questioning or hesitation. This was what aggravated the problems Kamal and Prem now faced. They just did not know.

CHAPTER VIII

In the station in Jullundur things had fallen into a well rehearsed routine. Now there was a slight creak as the door to the station master's cabin was opened cautiously and Sunny came in with a broad grin, which proclaimed satisfaction at a responsibility well taken care of. "The train has gone," he said, as if reporting that he had completed an assignment. "Very good," said Chote Ram, and meant it. "Another will come in 30 minutes and we can send that off too." He smiled at Sunny with genuine affection and got one of Sunny's lop sided grins. He nodded his head in agreement and perched in his corner waiting for further instructions. An unusual bond had emerged between Chote Ram and Sunny. Although they did not converse much, Sunny had taken to coming in every day and sitting in his corner quietly. It was as if he instinctively knew that in Chote Ram he had someone who would protect him.

To Chote Ram he was a mystery which had suddenly descended on him. Why God had chosen him of all people to look after this boy was something he would never know. But he knew with a certainty that it was his duty to see that Sunny got some food everyday and a place to curl up on the platform at night. He realized that the boy was not normal in the way the other boys his age were. If left to fend for himself he would soon fall prey to those who were ever watchful for just such opportunities. The boy had a wistful charm and a never failing smile for him. He reminded Chote Ram of his dog at home. He had the same trusting eyes and an utterly innocent look. So, what could he do but become an unwilling godfather.

Sunny watched Chote Ram intently and with great seriousness until feeling uncomfortable under the silent gaze, Chote Ram told him to go and have some lunch. Taking out two rupees he gave it to Sunny. "Tell the *puri wallah* to give you some *puris*" he said. After that first day when he had felt somehow compelled to feed him, he had not repeated his offer. Briju, the *puri wallah*, would curse him

82

but would finally part with the *puri*s and perhaps a generous dollop of spicy potato curry as well. Two rupees for what he charged five normally. He would have preferred that Sunny ask Briju himself but of course the boy could not or would not do this simple asking. Another mystery. He knew that Briju would do his bidding if he had asked, even if reluctantly. Hadn't he done enough favors even to the extent of seeing that his favorite and most profitable place on the platform was protected from other food sellers? But this Sunny would not ask for food. It was a most peculiar thing. Here he was obviously starving but he would not steal food like some of the other boys did nor beg for it!! A strange dignity in one who had no home and no family.

So, it was a two rupee note every afternoon. It was certain that Sunny would never know that Briju paid himself for this in many different ways. It also helped Chote Ram indirectly because Briju had the ears of many people on that platform and was an experienced master of platform politics, so that Chote Ram always knew where trouble was brewing and who was behind it. Sometimes Briju would even send a plateful of hot *puri*s to Chote Ram's house round the corner. This was particularly useful to mellow Saroj his wife whenever he was very late getting home. So the investment of two rupees a day was not lost since it brought in rich dividends. It was just that it was so intriguing.

CHAPTER IX

Bintu was Briju's helper. He was always on the lookout for Sunny to come for his two rupees worth of *puri*s. It was a welcome change. He enjoyed fooling this newcomer and got much satisfaction out of his discomfiture. Whenever Sunny came up to the *puri* stall Bintu would deliberately make no signs of recognition. He knew that Sunny would stand silently with the money clutched in his hand and would wait to be noticed. This irked Bintu. Who the hell did he think he was, this fellow who could not beg? He had seen Sunny go hungry many a time. If he could not get something to eat, he just curled up on his bench and slept.

Bintu caught himself thinking about Sunny many times. Who was he and where did he come from? Briju voiced the opinion of many on that platform. He thought that the boy had come from a good family. That explained why he could not bring himself to beg. In fact he did not know how to beg. Bintu snorted with laughter at this. He knew what hunger could make you do. Now, before Briju could chide him for being unkind to Sunny, he turned to him and said as if seeing him just then "*Arre*. Sunny. It's you. Why don't you say something *dost*? Just standing there like some silly girl too shy to speak up." Briju guffawed loudly and Sunny smiled, although he had a faint idea that he was the cause of their laughter. Bintu, good humor restored pulled out a generous bundle of *puri*s from under the leaves covering them and plunked it down in Sunny's hand. He pocketed the two rupees and turned to get a bowl of hot potato bhaji with a helping of hot green chilies for free. Once the whole packet was in his hand Sunny smiled politely and said in English "Thank You". This really broke up Bintu. "*Sala*," he said to anyone who would listen, "this *lallu* cannot even speak properly, but he says Thank You in English, *Sala*." The small audience that had gathered around Sunny and Bintu by now, laughed in loud appreciation. Sunny joined in the general laughter and loved the reaction this had. He was happy since he was the center of attention. He had made

Bintu happy and this gave Sunny a sense of achievement. "Thank you" he said again, bobbing his head in a manner which he had picked up, knowing that it would set everyone laughing again, which it did. He felt wonderful. These were his friends and he belonged here.

But Bintu was not finished with Sunny. "Listen to him now" he invited the interested group around them. "He cannot even say 'Rr', do you know that?" To Sunny he said loudly, "*Arre*, Sunny *Bhaiya*, what is this thing called?" He had an old stale chapatti in his hand. Sunny knew what it was. He replied at once. "That's a Noti", he said. The group dissolved in merriment. "Noti, Noti" they chanted. It was true that Sunny could not pronounce the letter 'R' and consequently used 'N' wherever there was an 'R'. But Bintu had something else in store for his audience. "What is your real name?" he asked. "NANJAN", said Sunny. "See," said Bintu. "*Sala* cannot even say his name but he says THANK YOU. He is an Englishman, a sahib from London." The group around Sunny and Bintu was enjoying every minute of this. One never knew what or how this strange fellow would react. But Sunny had had enough and he was hungry.

He walked away to his favorite bench near the third pillar, closest to the entrance from where he could see people in the streets, as well as keep an eye on whatever was happening on his platform. He ate ravenously. Six *puri*s did not take long to finish. Walking to the basin he washed his hands and mouth at the water tap. Hunger assuaged for the moment he looked around for a place to sleep. The bench he had been sitting on was still empty. At this time of the day, between trains, it usually was a comparatively quieter time. He knew that when the train came in the noise would wake him up. So it was safe to sleep now. He would not miss anything. Stretching out on the bench he belched loudly and settled down to sleep, oblivious of the eyes watching him.

Bintu could not bring himself to keep away from Sunny. Watching him eat and then settle down to sleep without a care in the world made him curious. He wondered what kind of a life he had led before he was pulled off the train. He had seen some glimpses of Sunny which hinted at a life very different to his own. He must have a family somewhere and perhaps they were searching for him. Nanjan. That meant his real name was Ranjan. Perhaps a big house with a bathroom and everything, judging from the way Sunny washed his hands and cleaned himself. He just had to find out more about him. Briju said the gods seemed to take care of Sunny. Perhaps he was right.

Bintu felt himself descending into a well of self-pity and shook himself out of it before he became maudlin. Ever since Sunny had so suddenly appeared on the platform, he had felt vague disquiet. He remembered how he himself came to be on platform No. 4. His mother had brought him there when he was about ten. He had waited in vain for her return. She never came back. If it had not been for Briju who had taken him home, he would perhaps be in the same situation in which Sunny found himself now. But it was no use thinking about the past. He tried never to think of his mother. Bintu had learnt that very early. No use at all. And anyway, as Briju kept telling him, you cannot change what had already happened. He sometimes wished he could share this with Sunny.

CHAPTER X

Bintu had time on his hands after each train pulled out of the station. Everything returned to normal. The tempo slowed down and everyone on the platform went back into a lethargy from which they roused themselves only when the next train came in. He walked over to where Sunny was sleeping and shook him awake.

Sunny was irritated. He disliked being woken up. Left to himself, he would lie stretched on his back for hours on end. But Bintu was not giving up easily. Sitting on the hard wooden bench next to Sunny, Bintu felt a sudden warm tenderness for Sunny he had rarely experienced before. He was genuinely sorry that he had made everyone laugh at him although Sunny himself did not seem to care about being made the butt of jokes. Perhaps he could make it up to him, he thought. He knew that Sunny had never gone out of the station. He would take him into town and show him the city. What a treat that would be. So, he kept shaking him until with a loud irritated shout, Sunny sat up.

"Bintu. Bintu. Stop shaking me," said a visibly annoyed Sunny.

"Come with me" said an unfazed Bintu. Sunny shook his head. He was in no mood to go anywhere. He looked with bleary sleep-filled eyes at the familiar world around him. He just wanted to go back to sleep and made ready to stretch out again. But Bintu, mind made up, was having none of it.

"Come, I will take you to the market," he said coaxingly. The magic word market activated him and he sat up grinning widely. "Yes. Yes." he said with enthusiasm to a now smiling Bintu. The market. He knew that in the market, you could get things to eat. There would be lots of shops and lots of people. Vague memories stirred in his mind of another market somewhere else. But he could neither identify the strange feelings which flooded him nor identify where and when he had visited other markets. Bintu and Sunny walked out of the station, happiness apparent on Sunny's face. He greeted everyone he knew by name. The *coolies* who had to sometimes wrestle with him to leave their passengers and their luggage alone, waved with smiling tolerance. The ticket collector at the gate who knew Sunny by sight let him go with a nod at his friendly greeting.

Once out into the open, Sunny stood still. Bintu wondered how long he had been on the platform without once coming out. The sight of the rows of taxis and the scooter rickshaws seemed to amaze him. He looked around as if he had never seen anything like this before. Walking on to the main road he wanted to stop at every store. Most tempting were the food stalls. Although the railway station had its share of these stalls the variety and sheer number of food items displayed in stall after stall was an irresistible draw. Bintu put his arm through Sunny's and tried to hurry him past. But at one of the sweet shops Bintu lost to Sunny's craving for anything sweet. At the sight of piles of *jalebis* oozing syrup, Sunny just stood with his mouth open. The longing in his eyes was apparent. Just looking at them made his mouth water. Bintu tried to pull him away. It was no use. He stood as if rooted to the spot. He pretended to walk away, sure that Sunny would come after him in panic at being left alone. This didn't work either. There was only one thing he could do now. He sighed. OK he decided. I will get him some *jalebis*. Digging out a crumpled note from his short khaki pants, which had seen better days, he ordered one rupees worth. He held it out to Sunny. "Here. Take this," he said, feeling a warm glow inside him as he saw Sunny's genuine smile of pleasure. He was about to help himself to one of the *jalebis* when Sunny turned away from Bintu and started tucking into them with gusto. "Thank you" said Sunny. Bintu laughed. "*Sala*" he said, as he adroitly whisked one *jalebi* off the leaf plate and stuffed it into his mouth before Sunny could react.

He put his arm over Sunny's shoulder and they walked together with no particular destination in mind. They went down the lane which led away from the railway station. Bintu allowed Sunny to stop at shops which interested him now that there were no more food shops in sight. One shop in particular fascinated both Sunny and Bintu. It had a large window which displayed some of the latest electronic equipment. The wide TV screens displayed there made Bintu exclaim in wonder. Did people really use things like this? But his interest shifted to Sunny when he pointed to a camcorder. It was obvious that Sunny really recognized something which was familiar to him. "*Bhaiya* has one like this he said" loudly grinning his lopsided grin. Bintu's mouth fell open in amazement. His mind raced furiously. If Sunny's *bhaiya* had one like this, then he must really belong to a rich family, he thought. But on second thoughts perhaps it was just Sunny. One never knew when to believe him. So, he laughed well naturedly.

"Sure. Sure." He said. "Perhaps you also have a big TV like that one" he said, pointing to a twenty eight inch screen.

"Yes" said Sunny at once. Bintu laughed and to show Sunny how funny what he said had been, he staggered about holding his stomach and laughing.

"Oh yes." he said. "You have a big, big TV, you have a big house, you have a big car, and you have everything don't you *SALA*? What are you doing in the station then *Sala*?"

Bintu was harsh without intending to be. In a remote corner of his mind he was thinking that Sunny perhaps did have all the things he knew he would never, ever possess. He had often seen and admired the cars which came to the station to drop or pick up people. He knew that getting into one of those was a very remote possibility. Even though he knew he was being unfair to Sunny, he could not stop taunting him and laughing. Sunny was confused. He knew that he had watched TV with his mother and father but was not sure where it was or when this had been. Vague pictures flashed through his mind. He saw *Bhaiya*. He saw his mother and his father and they all sat watching TV. He had glimpses of the room his mother sat in. The green and yellow TV cover his mother had stitched floated across his mind. What was that? Where was this? He had a vague sense of a house and a garden. He remembered a music system similar to the one he had seen. He remembered people who had looked after him and gave him good things to eat. But he did not know where they were or where he was. It was somewhere very far away he knew and it made him angry and uncomfortable. He looked at Bintu and he clamped his mouth shut tight. He looked grim and unhappy. Now that he was in a situation where he did not know what he was supposed to know, Sunny became quiet and withdrawn. He wanted to get away from this place of memories over which he had no control.

Turning away from the shop window Sunny ran blindly down the lane he saw in front of him. Bintu was appalled at the sudden change in Sunny. One single remark and Sunny was upset. He had well naturedly withstood such situations before even joining in the laughter. What was wrong with him now? This new Sunny made him uneasy. But it was time to be getting back to the station. He ran after Sunny pulling him by the arm.

"*Arre. Arre. Arre,*" he said. "What is the matter with you? Come back. Come back. It is time we got back to the station."

But Sunny was in a strange mood. He could not tell anyone about what he felt or why he felt the way he did it. It made him melancholy and without knowing why he started crying. He felt an overwhelming sense of loss and all he could do was sob. Great shudders of sobs shook him with an agony he could not put into words or express in any way.

Bintu had no way of knowing what had caused this explosion of crying. So he followed Sunny bothered and perplexed. "*Arre. Bhai*" he kept saying. "What happened *Yaar*?" He tried bribing Sunny. "Do you want some more *jalebis*?" he asked, hoping that Sunny would not say "Yes." But Sunny would only sob. He looked so pathetic walking along the dirt road, wiping his nose and his face with his shirt sleeve, that Bintu felt close to tears himself. But they had come to the end of the lane now and in front of them was a big drain. It was the town sewer, open and covered with gray slime. Blue, white and green plastic bags dotted here and there. Reeds grew along the sides and the long green stems made a contrast to the sluggish water in the sewer. A gentle grassy slope led down to it. Sunny scrambled down the slope and threw himself down on the grass. Though patchy and green only in some places it was clean. Not the best of places to be, thought Bintu but the grass was cool and pleasant and there was peace and quite here. Sinking down beside his friend, he rolled over on his stomach and pillowed his face in his hands. Sunny's crying gradually became sniffles and seeing Bintu on his stomach, he promptly imitated him though tears still wet his cheeks. Bintu smiled in approval. Sunny smiled back. He was back to normal. Whatever had made him cry so agonizingly forgotten for the moment.

Never one to lose an opportunity Bintu thought he should make use of this moment. Seeing him recognize the costly equipment in the shop had been an eye opener.

"So, Sunny," he said, after a companionable silence, "Where did you come from?"

"From the railway station" said Sunny without hesitation.

Bintu hooted with laughter "I mean before that. Where is your home?"

Sunny was silent. Where was his home? "*Arre, Budhu*, which city? Bombay, Calcutta, Delhi…?"

"Delhi" said Sunny firmly. For this knew.

Bintu looked at him in astonishment. "Delhi" said Sunny again, shaking his head confidently as if he had found the answer to some problem that had been worrying him for a long time.

"Delhi" echoed Bintu. So, that explained many things about Sunny. How he seemed to be used to traffic and people and knew about water taps and washing himself with soap every day. Bintu recalled how he had seen Sunny trying to wash his T-shirt one day. It was obvious he had not done so before. Bintu had had to help him out and show him how to rub the soap on to the shirt. It also explained his polite manners and his everlasting "Thank yous" and his patient waiting near the *puri* stall. Waiting to be given rather than ask.

Bintu's interest awakened. "Do you have a mother?"

Sunny nodded his head again. "Yes."

"And Daddy," in a matter of fact way.

Bintu was amazed that Sunny did remember. He did something unexpected now. Before he could ask more questions, Sunny started to talk, words merging into each other in his urgency to get it out. He was like a rain water drain thought Bintu, which gushed with water after the monsoons and would stop only after the rains had stopped. He was not wrong because Sunny had tapped into some hidden reservoir of long buried memories and they came out now all together, jumbled anyhow but giving him a tremendous feeling of release so that he just had to say whatever came into his mind. Bintu kept nodding his head several times to show Sunny that he was listening and was interested in what he was saying. It did make fascinating listening.

"I have a music system at home," said Sunny. "I have cassettes."

To Bintu who had only seen a music system in the shop windows, this revelation caused intense and a momentary jealousy. He talked about things which made no sense to Bintu. About his school where he made paper bags. A school which taught him paper bag making? Bintu had to laugh. What kind of a school taught this? But it was all very muddled. Sunny was talking about his home in Delhi and his life now in Jullundur as if they were all happening at the same time. He went back and forth saying things about cars and motor cycles and school and even names of people. None of this made any sense to Bintu. But one thing was clear, that Sunny was actually the son of some well-off people in Delhi. Should he tell Chote Ram? Briju perhaps? But almost as soon as he thought of it he squashed the idea. He would wait until he got more out of Sunny.

But Sunny stopped talking as suddenly as he had started. All further efforts to get him to continue failed. Sunny would not have been able to say what he wanted to say even if he had wished to. Bintu shook his head in frustration. He was tired of Sunny. He was OK for a laugh and to sit around with but a companion with whom he could make conversation? Definitely not. He sighed as he realized this.

"Come on Sunny," he said with resignation. "It's time we got back to the station. Briju will be looking for me. There is another train due now."

Sunny got up immediately. He knew that without him there the trains would not move. That was his work and he had to get back to his work as well. Running down the street with Sunny behind him, Bintu did not see the group of people across the road. But Sunny did. Insatiably curious, he stopped to look. The crowd pressing in behind him enveloped him completely. On the pavement sat a snake charmer with an open basket in front of him. A huge cobra reared its head and puffed itself out darting its thin black tongue in and out. Sunny stood rooted with eyes fixed on the snake. The snake charmer was playing on a strange looking instrument. Sunny wanted one like that. He was sure he could also play on it like the snake charmer.

He turned around to ask Bintu if he could get one like that but Bintu was nowhere in sight. The snake charmer also had finished his show and was packing up his basket pushing the snake inside with the tip of his flute. The crowd began to thin. Those who could, threw coins into the basket lid. The people on the street who lounged about looked at him with interest. Sunny was anxious now and not finding Bintu beside him he started running back to the railway station.

He had first run and then walked for what seemed to him a long time. The railway station was nowhere in sight. It did not occur to Sunny that he might have made a mistake in the direction he took. He just walked along thinking that he would eventually arrive at the railway station. He was getting tired. So when he saw a large compound with many trees which were shady and looked cool he did not hesitate going in. Sunny walked into the compound through the open gate and sat down under the tree. The compound Sunny had entered was that of an old church. A beautiful building built in the colonial style by the British. It had a very large portico, steps going up to a beautiful and huge carved wooden door. Sunny saw none of this. All he wanted now was to rest for some time before Bintu came to find him and take him back.

CHAPTER XI

Father Paul, forty and balding and Pastor in charge of the Methodist Mission Church in the old part of Jullundur town, had been sitting cooped up at his desk most of the afternoon. He was preparing the sermon for the Sunday service the next day. But inspiration was lacking. He had his text but could find nothing new to say. He felt hot and bothered. Lately he had started questioning his very existence as pastor. The youthful zeal which had propelled him into the often unenviable life of a preacher had long since been replaced with resignation. He felt the familiar sagging of spirits and a lethargy which came with the knowledge that nothing he could do or say would change the congregation he had been given. Whatever he preached, there were always those who compared him with the Rev. Ernest David, the last pastor who had been shipped home to his home church in Surrey with acute stomach infection. The best of medical treatment available in Jullundur had had no effect on the good Reverend. But people remembered him with awe and with some affection. They remembered his sermons which were often above the understanding of most of the congregation but which by its very incomprehension proved its worth. They remembered his clipped British accent and his unfailing courtesy to even the lowest of the natives. The Christmas trees and the decorations brought all the way from London and which rested now lovingly wrapped in individual pieces of colored paper in separate boxes in the vestry drew great crowds for the Christmas service. It was worth travelling great distances just to be able to see the glass reindeer, the jolly red Santa Clauses, the ethereally beautiful silver and foil angels. They were examined and exclaimed over and remembered long after Christmas was a memory. His wife Miriam had been a source of great comfort and many wonderful recipes to the women. Rev. Paul knew and understood that in comparison he paled drastically. But the church was his responsibility and he was the one chosen to inspire and lead the Christian population of Jullundur to turn their eyes towards Heaven.

Today inspiration was far from him. He stood up in desperation and walked to the window. He was not at his best when he was writing his sermons. It always made him irritated. Those who listened when he preached, did so out of habit and years of long practice made them adept at switching off and on as they wished. Rev. Paul knew this and in fact appreciated that his loyal parishioners resorted to this rather than question him on his sermons or criticize him on his choice of text and scripture. Except of course some old biddies who came in late smelling of perfume which mingled with a strong whiff of their *aloo paratha* breakfast and said things like, "When Ernest was here…" or "Ernest would not have said it this way…" Although it usually left him defeated he continued to try and did indeed take a lot of trouble with the preparation of his sermons.

The mission church was small and Rev. Paul was usually satisfied with the way his destiny had landed him in Jullundur. A spacious house to stay in and a congregation which was not too demanding but was not too much trouble either. He was not married, having chosen the Church as his vocation. He often said to himself and to others, "What else could a man of God ask for?" Nevertheless, sometimes he felt vague discomforts. Recently he had taken to thinking nostalgically of opportunities lost and a sense of getting on in years with nothing to show for his forty odd years of life on this earth. He yearned for some mission which would come his way. Something which would make him feel that he had done a worthwhile job. People would remember him for that. "Do you remember Rev. Paul?" they would tell one another when they met in their elegant drawing rooms. "He was the one who did…" Here his mind drew a blank. Did what? What could he do shut away here in a town which did not boast of a large Christian population. As the familiar thoughts went through his mind this Saturday afternoon he stared moodily out of the window.

Preoccupied with himself he did not at first notice the reclining figure of someone stretched out under the gulmohar tree in the front compound. When he did realize that it was a stranger and not the *mali* taking a nap, his curiosity was instantly aroused. He went at a fast clip out of the door of his small study cum office, his white robe billowing behind him and ran to the sleeping figure. He was genuinely concerned. Was it someone hurt? Dying? He saw a young man fast asleep with his mouth open and arms flung in wide abandon. A strange looking young man. Rev. Paul had seen children like this at the Home for the Mentally Challenged run by the Sisters of Charity. Was he perhaps one of them? But no, he answered himself, the sisters looked after only girls. This young man had to be from somewhere else.

He shook the boy awake. Smiling, so as not to alarm the boy, he put his arm on his shoulder. "Are you lost?" asked Rev. Paul, expecting an answer. But the boy, rudely woken up, looked surly and angry. He would only look at him dully with lips compressed in a stubborn straight line. Rev. Paul continued to question him with the hope that he would get some information which would help him to take a decision. But nothing he could say brought any kind of an intelligent response.

So he did the only sensible thing to do. He took him into his house and making him comfortable went into his neat little dining room to look for something to drink. Perhaps something to eat as well. Sunny understood what the man was proposing to do and once inside the cool drawing room felt immediately better. He looked around him and seeing the TV and the music system in the corner went towards it and started looking at the pile of audio cassettes which was stacked neatly by the side. When Rev. Paul came in with a cold glass of sweet *lassi* which he had fortunately found in the fridge and was to have been part of his midmorning snack, he found the boy engrossed with the music system. His first reaction was one of alarm. The TV and his music system were both old but the result of many months of planning and saving. It was the one source of recreation and was a prized possession. But this boy seemed to know what he was doing. Seeing Rev. Paul standing there with the glass of *lassi* in his hand, Sunny smiled with evident delight and said with the characteristic shake of his head "I have one like this in my house." Rev. Paul smiled now with relief and asked the obvious question "Where is your house?" Even though he knew his house was in Delhi, for some inexplicable reason Sunny decided he was not going to say anything else. Sunny did have vague memories which sometimes persisted but often just flitted across his mind. In a way it was fortunate that Sunny did not remember much except when events and situations brought about a sudden flash of remembrance as had happened in the market with Bintu. But it did not really matter thought Rev. Paul. This boy was obviously tired and hungry and had been sent to him to look after.

Inside the cool interior of the old mission bungalow, Sunny settled himself on the maroon cushion which covered the hard angular projections of the large cane chair in the room. He looked around dispassionately. He was not too interested in the house or the man who had asked him to come in. When Rev Paul offered him the glass of *lassi* he accepted it gratefully with a polite "Thank You" and gulped it down thirstily. He put the glass back carefully on the small cane table in front of him.

Preliminaries done, Rev. Paul welcomed the distraction this sudden intrusion had provided him. He started asking questions once again but had to give up in frustration. The only thing he got out of this boy was that his name was Sunny and that he lived on the railway station. This bit of information however told Rev. Paul quite a bit. All he had to do now was to take Sunny back to the railway station and deliver him to his family. But he was also experienced in the way such unexpected events had of backfiring on one and creating unasked-for trouble. The case of the girl who had run away from the *Nari Niketan* and landed up on his doorstep was fresh in his mind. He had become embroiled in an unnecessary and time consuming controversy with the authorities of the *Nari Niketan* and the police. He had no wish to get entangled again. So he rang up the station master of the railway station. After all, since the boy seemed to know no other home than the platform of the Jullundur Station, it was an obvious and logical course of action.

What Rev. Paul learnt through his call to Chote Ram changed the course of his life. It was also the cause of the best ever sermon that he had ever delivered. A sermon that astounded and delighted the discerning among his flock and gave him a reputation which established him, much to his delight as a speaker at many small functions in the city of Jullundur.

When Bintu realized that Sunny was no longer with him, he had come running in breathlessly straight to Chote Ram. He was sobbing and truly sorry that he had not been able to bring Sunny back safely to the railway station. With tears running down his face and his nose blocked with the crying, he looked for all the world as if some major disaster had befallen him. He managed to gasp out how he had kept his eyes on Sunny all the time but that Sunny had somehow managed to lose himself. He had cried himself hoarse shouting out his name and running up and down the street where they had gone down to the lane and the *nullah*. It had been no use. He had lost Sunny. Chote Ram was taken aback at this display by Bintu, who had till then a reputation of a tough guy, small as he was. The others on the platform had offered to go out and search. But Chote Ram said no. It would be a waste of time. He knew that searching for Sunny was a major exercise which he could not undertake. There was no saying where and with whom he may have gone. So, he wisely refrained from sending out the group of boys from the platform, who sensing drama and a relief from the boredom of their daily life were eager to run around the streets looking for Sunny. But Chote Ram was sad. He would miss Sunny and knew exactly why Bintu was so heart broken. There had been something about that boy that endeared him to everyone he met. He knew that he would wonder everlastingly what had happened to him.

When Rev. Paul's phone call had come in the late afternoon, he had little difficulty in identifying that the boy the Reverend was talking about was none other than Sunny. He gave Rev. Paul a detailed story of what Sunny had been doing on the station platform and how he had arrived there in the first place. Dates were vague but both Rev. Paul and Chote Ram knew that asking Sunny would yield no real answers.

He was excited at hearing that Sunny had landed himself in the care of the revered at the church and truly relieved that Sunny had come to no harm but had once again succeeded on falling on his feet as it were. He had always been apprehensive that Sunny would one day get into trouble if he continued to live on the platform. He also felt quite irrationally that it was his responsibility to keep a zealous guard over him. It was because of this that he took what was a wholly reasonable decision to the problem of what to do with Sunny. He asked Rev. Paul to keep Sunny with him and train him to become his helper. He knew from the way Sunny had picked up the train timings and the waving on and off of the trains that if someone took the time and the trouble to teach Sunny, he could pick up many skills. He kept Rev. Paul riveted with his stories about how Sunny had appointed himself his unofficial deputy. Rev. Paul chuckled heartily.

When Chote Ram told him how Sunny's strange pride would not let him steal food but made him stand patiently waiting for handouts which he would accept gratefully, Rev. Paul could guess at the kind of life Sunny must have had before he came to the railway station. He nodded in solemn affirmation when Chote Ram shared with him that Sunny obviously belonged to a cultured family which had brought him up in luxury but with strict principles. Bintu had also told him some of the things Sunny had said about his home in Delhi and he told Rev. Paul about this. This was a lead which Rev. Paul could follow, suggested Chote Ram since as a priest he could do so easily. There was much laughter and a mutual delight between the two men. They had never met but were both appointed Sunny's guardians by circumstances which were not of their doing.

After his long conversation with Rev. Paul, Chote Ram sent for Bintu anticipating the delight that the good news would give Bintu.

"Be happy. Be happy." he said to Bintu, the excitement apparent in his voice and the way he sat shaking his legs in quick jerky movements. "Sunny has actually found himself someone who will look after him," he told Bintu expecting relief and grateful smiles. But in spite of the earlier reaction and the heartbreaking tears, Bintu's immediate reaction was one of his own loss rather than concern for Sunny. What would he do now with no Sunny to while away the free time between trains.

But all he did was nod his head slowly several times and walk away. He was happy but a conflict of emotions fought for space in his heart. Was he happy for Sunny but sad that he also did not find someone to look after him? He did not know the answer himself.

When he had finished his long conversation with Chote Ram, Rev. Paul sat looking at Sunny, now demolishing a plateful of bread and jam. Sunny who adored jam and had been deprived of it for many long months was touchingly grateful for what Rev. Paul had made available. As he watched him eat, a plan was slowly taking shape in Rev. Paul's mind. A sense of purpose gradually filled him. He recalled the loved and familiar words from the bible. "If you do this unto the least of my brothers, you do it unto me."

CHAPTER XII

The third Sunday of the month of May was a day which would live long in the memory of Rev. Paul. The summer heat had been at its highest. But the faithful had come. The heat outside was like a palpable shimmering veil. The congregation gradually settled down and the coughs and rustles of sarees finally quietened. The faithful sat in preparation for a one hour long service which they would have to go through, but grateful for the peaceful and cool interior of the church.

This Sunday, Rev. Paul's sermon had been inspired by meeting Sunny. It was as if God had said, "Paul, I am sending you Sunny. Look after him and let him be an inspiration and the cause you are searching for." A delighted Rev. Paul had wasted no time in scurrying to his study and putting pen to paper had written out a sermon which dealt with compassion. With the opportunities God sends us every day, if only we are alert to his ways, to test us and yes, to reward us if we do his will. What was His will? To serve. Serve with single minded devotion and with no thought of any kind of material returns. Surely God would see and decide what their reward should be.

Many in the congregation were delighted at the new Rev. Paul. One who spoke with conviction and confidence. There were those of course who wondered loudly if he had stumbled upon Ernest's sermons and simply passed it off as his own. But then there are people like this in any parish and we are not concerned with them.

Sunny, innocent of the change he had brought about in the life of Rev Paul settled down quite happily to his new comforts. He now slept on a cot with a soft mattress. His meals were regular. He liked Rev. Paul and the mealtimes when Rev. Paul would tell him about the city and ask him many questions about himself. He tried his best to give answers to this kind man who was so nice to him but could not always do so. Most of all he enjoyed the time spent with the *mali* watering the plants and the large vegetable garden behind the mission house.

Life for Sunny and Rev. Paul went smoothly. They met at meal times and Rev. Paul was always happy to listen seriously to whatever Sunny had to say. Sunny had now settled down to his new life as comfortably as he had done at the railway station. He liked his new surroundings. He liked sitting with Hari, the old *mali* under the giant gulmohar tree and watch him light up his *beedi*. He had tried to wheedle a *beedi* out of Hari.

"Just one" he said pleadingly. "You can smoke and so can I." But old Hari had thrown up his hands in horror and ruffled his hair. "*Na Baba. Na*" he said very firmly and that was that. But Sunny was not so easily deterred. He wanted a *beedi*. Opportunity came his way soon one hot afternoon when Hari was gently snoring under the gulmohar tree. Creeping up close to Hari he took out his bundle of *beedis* and the match box. He sat cross legged near Hari and inhaled. Not able to do so properly at first he sat there enjoying the puffing but not really taking it in. Until suddenly an extra-large inhalation choked him with acrid fumes and he jumped up spluttering and coughing and clutching his throat. Hari sat up in alarm but when he had taken in the sight of Sunny coughing away, he just sat there and roared with laughter.

This is what Manjit heard from her vantage point in the kitchen. From there she could see the long stretch of road leading to the garden gate and she could see both Sunny and old Hari. Manjit, the live-in cook and maid came with the mission house. She had seen many pastors come and go for the past thirty years at least. She had grown with the church and knew more than anyone else about the church and its early history. She had successfully trained each of the pastors and their families to her way of doing things and knew their innermost secrets. She was indispensable to Rev. Paul. She had kept house for a long line of pastors of the Methodist Church of Jullundur, both British and Indian and other interim occupants and could tell you stories both droll and sad when she was in the mood. She was generally liked by most people except for the odd pastors who brought their wives along and expected her to change her routine to suit theirs. Mild Rev. Paul listened politely to Manjit and her advice on the many small problems that beset him. Right from treating him with an infusion of *tulsi* leaves for his cold, to meeting his visitors when he was unable to do so, Manjit as everyone knew, was the one to watch out for. It would never do to annoy old Manjit.

Seeing Sunny from the window and old Hari sitting on the ground laughing, she rushed out. Taking in the situation in one glance she glared at Hari and the look said "it is all your fault." Hari shook his head to her unspoken accusation. But Sunny had got over his fit of coughing now and it was obvious that he had not enjoyed the experience.

"Go inside and drink some water." Manjit directed him. But the incident gave her an idea. It was brilliant and one which would benefit everyone. Most of all it would benefit her husband who spent long hours polishing the richly inlaid brass vessels which held the flowers for the Sunday morning services.

"Why do you feed this boy for no reason?" she demanded shrilly of Rev. Paul after he had finished his dinner. "What good is he if you do not train him for some honest work?"

Rev. Paul had to agree. What Manjit said made a lot of sense. So during a casual conversation at breakfast he asked Sunny if he would be able to do more than just walk around the garden with the *mali* though of course even that was a valuable help to the *mali*, he hastened to add. To Sunny it made no difference at all where he worked and he agreed without hesitation, shaking his head and smiling. "How about polishing the brassware in the church?" asked Rev. Paul now, happy that Sunny had agreed so readily. Sunny could polish the brass cross and the brass altar railings he thought. Manjit was delighted too. It would give her husband, who now did this chore, some free time and he could then help her in the kitchen.

Rev. Paul's reasons were different. It had been Sunny after all who had come to him so suddenly and in such a miraculous way and it would be a nice gesture to introduce him to the church, even if at first, it would be through the cleaning chores. Thus it was that Sunny began his new life. He was given the specific responsibility of polishing the cross which stood on the altar and the railings that separated the altar from the nave. Sunny, as always when he enjoyed something, did this with great enthusiasm and energy and whatever could be polished in the church shone with a luster every Sunday morning showing ample evidence of his hard work. It was not lost on the congregation and many of them complimented Rev. Paul in the way he had given shelter to Sunny. Soon, Sunny graduated from alter railings to the big brass vases with the intricate carvings and which needed every crevice and scroll to be laboriously cleaned. It was something which fascinated Sunny and he loved to see how the dark dull brass came to life and blazed with light. And all because of him. Somewhere along the way he learnt to imitate Rev. Paul even to the inflection of the voice when he said "Thanks be to God." It delighted Rev. Paul and Sunny knew this and would say it whenever he happened to be inside the church and whether or not it suited the occasion.

Gradually a routine was established. Sunny and Rev. Paul would breakfast together and when Rev. Paul went into his small study to pray and read the bible, Sunny was often his companion. It was to him that Rev. Paul laid bare his soul knowing that it was safe and would be forgotten almost immediately. But it served a cathartic purpose. His dreams, his problems which prevented him from reaching his goals and even his confessions of various sins which he had committed or thought he had committed would all come out at the morning sessions together. Sunny would listen to every single word with the most careful attention and would nod his head in agreement whenever he was asked if something was not so. He felt safe with Rev. Paul and seldom interrupted his soliloquies sensing in some uncanny way that he was a crucial part of these daily meetings.

It was on one of these days that Rev. Paul introduced the subject of his old motorcycle which had been lying unused in the garage. It was the only mode of transport that Rev. Paul possessed. But it needed to be cleaned regularly and this he had not done for some time. He took Sunny along to the garage to take a look at his motorbike. To his surprise and delight, Sunny laughed out loudly with real pleasure and lovingly ran his hand over the bike. He shook his head in his characteristic gesture of approval which indicated that he was familiar with a motorbike. Rev. Paul of course had no idea of the many times that Sunny had cleaned his brother's motorbike back in Delhi and had received either chocolates for a job well done or a rap on the back of his head.

Seeing Sunny so delighted with the bike now, Rev. Paul asked him if he could clean this as well. Sunny agreed with alacrity. So this was added to his duties. Clean the brassware in the church every Saturday, the bike every morning and help the *mali* with the watering of the garden every evening. But the garden routine was flexible and he often just wandered around looking at the flowers and the *mali* would know that today he would get no help from Sunny. But when Sunny was in the mood to work, both the *mali* and Manjit's husband would wait for Sunny *baba* to come and do his bit of work. Never mind the times when he over watered or pulled out radishes instead of grass or used up more polish than the church had used in the past month. All in all it was a happy time for both Sunny and the Mission Church and in particular for Rev. Paul who used Sunny's story of how God looks after his own in many ways.

Perhaps life would have just meandered along for both Rev. Paul and Sunny if they had been left to live their lives as they wanted to. But this was not to be. Chote Ram had been careful about not revealing Sunny's whereabouts to Bintu and the others. He did not want him back on the platform and definitely not back in his life complicating it. So fate took another way.

Some of the young men who came to church did so on motorbikes. Some of them came to show off to the young girls they eyed from afar since it was not done to be seen talking to any one girl in particular. It was not good for the girl and not good for the boy. In fact it could land the boy into a lot of trouble. So, while anxious mothers swept the eligible young men with their eyes every Sunday morning the bolder girls dared to look directly at them during the service. This was possible because the men and women sat on opposite sides of the church facing each other. This arrangement which the Rev. Ernest David had approved caused more trouble than it prevented according to Rev. Paul. Instead of keeping the boys and girls away from each other, coy smiles flashed across the sanctum sanctorum establishing unspoken communications. Sometimes this worked out just fine. But then sometimes it did not and when such instances happened, it caused much unpleasantness and agony for everyone and particularly Rev. Paul since both the parties of the boy and the girl felt that somehow, being the pastor, he should have known what was happening during his sermons.

After being introduced to Rev. Paul's motorbike, Sunny considered himself adept at cleaning motorbikes in general. He had started feeling an expert's pride and concern for all motorbikes. If thoughts of his brother's bike ever came to him he was unable to share it with anyone. On a particular Sunday, Sunny who usually strayed into the church and strayed out again as he wished was drawn to the motorbikes parked in a row rather than to go into the church building.

One of the motorbikes in the row was all spit and polish. Sunny looked at it with approval. Lovingly he passed his hand over its body and seat and putting both hands on the handle bars felt the hardness of the leather coverings and laughed at the way the decorative tassels dangling from the handlebars shook in rhythm to his twisting them. It was when he was doing this that the last benediction was given and the people came pouring out into the compound.

Robert, to whom the bike belonged was new to Jullundur. His family had been here just for the last couple of months. However he did know of Sunny and how he helped Rev. Paul in the maintenance of the church. The bike was new and his great pride and joy. Maybe he could be excused for what he did or maybe God had other plans for Sunny and it was time for him to move on. Seeing Sunny standing with his hands on the handlebars, Robert's fear was that Sunny would kick it to life any second now and roar away. Even as his rational mind told him that Sunny may not know how to drive and perhaps had no intention of doing so, he had rushed from the door of the church with such a fierce yell that he startled people still coming out of the church and made every head turn towards Sunny and the hurtling figure of Robert.

Later there were many versions of what had happened. Aunty Elsie swore that she had seen white figures hovering over Sunny who had helped him to escape the fury of Robert. Most people however just saw Robert, insane with anger throw himself at a wholly unprepared Sunny who was sent flying into the air by a well calculated fist on his head. Rev. Paul was shaken and angry. He came flying out of the church, cassock ballooning out behind him in the wind. Truly like an avenging angel, thought the onlookers admiringly.

Like the other time when he was hit by Bhima and Rattan, Sunny never knew what had hit him or why he had been hit. He had been picked up immediately and rushed into the mission house while people stayed gingerly away from Robert. His first fury over, Robert had realized too late that Sunny was only twisting the handle bars back and forth. He had no intention of staying on to find out what had happened to Sunny. People made way for him as he went roaring out of the church grounds, the motorbike revved up to maximum and sounding as if it was expressing the fury that its master, Robert, had felt. Rev. Paul heard patiently the different versions people had to tell him. It was finally the old *mali* who had been close by and had seen the whole thing who clarified things for everyone.

"Poor Sunny *Baba* was not doing anything at all" he told an enthralled audience. "It was a deplorable incident" he said and everyone agreed solemnly.

"To hit a poor defenseless boy and that too inside the church compound. This is surely a sin."

"What were the young coming to these days?" some of them wondered loudly. It was all the violence on TV which was now available to anyone and anywhere.

While Sunny was being administered to by an anxious Rev. Paul and a tongue-clicking and concerned Manjit, many of the congregation stayed on, waiting to hear that everything was alright with Sunny. One of them who happened to be a doctor had personally examined Sunny and had declared that he would have a massive headache but the bruise on his head was not something to worry about. He had cleaned the small cut and dabbed some tincture of iodine on it. Sunny had screamed when it smarted, making everyone nervous and had started saying unintelligible things. His sobs were heartrending.

It was this incident which made Rev. Paul rethink the wisdom of keeping Sunny with him. While the dressing was being done he had very clearly understood two or three words that Sunny was shouting. One was "Mummy." So, Sunny did remember his mother and even longed for her, though it perhaps surfaced only when there had been some provocation which made Sunny sad or upset. He decided that he should make very serious attempts to trace Sunny's parents and inform them that he was safe with him. He even dared to hope that he could talk them into allowing him to keep Sunny with him. He would find a small job for him and pay him a nominal salary. He could have his own bank account and could certainly be taught to operate it. Rev. Paul found himself comforted with this thought.

Thus it was that the next day found the Rev. Paul sitting in the rickety chair in the station master's cabin in Jullundur railway station. Chote Ram felt honored and important to be thus sought out by this man of God. He sat listening with rapt attention to what the Rev. was telling him about Sunny. He was delighted that Sunny had learnt to polish the brass inside the church as well as the motorbikes. This only showed that he had been right and that the boy had skills which could be coaxed out of him with patient and gentle handling. He felt justified in having taken the decision not to divulge Sunny's whereabouts even to Bintu.

Now in collective wisdom Rev. Paul and Chote Ram decided that the best way to trace Sunny's parents were to put an advertisement in the English language papers. To Rev. Paul's suggestion that they share the cost of the advertisement Chote Ram agreed. His hesitation had been only for a split second when a vision of his enraged wife Saroj, who would never have agreed to that, had sped through his mind and disappeared. The advertisement, when it appeared was read with great interest by the locals in Jullundur and particularly the members of Rev. Paul's congregation. But even if it was read in the other editions of the newspaper which both Rev. Paul and Chote Ram had selected with great care and after much discussion about the extent of its readership outside Jullundur and the costs involved, it was doubtful whether it evoked anything but the most cursory interest. When days passed into weeks and there was no reply, Rev. Paul began to think that it was truly God's wish that he be the sole guardian and protector of Sunny.

Things began to settle down once more after this flurry of activity. Sunny was back at his regular chores inside the church and in the large compound and kitchen garden. The only note of sadness was the complete absence of young Robert from the church services. Rev. Paul sometimes felt that perhaps it was ordained that he should lose Robert and find Sunny. One Sunday Rev. Paul was busy with some of his parishioners in his study. Looking out of the window, he saw Sunny, as usual stretched out under his favorite tree. Sunny had been his ward and helper for a good six months now and life had taken on new meaning for Rev. Paul. Smiling at the many memories the sight of Sunny always brought him he turned away from the window. Sunny turned over on to his stomach lazily. He was content lying there in the shade of the old gulmohar tree. From his place under the tree he could see the traffic on the road outside. Like many times before, he felt suddenly lost and lonely though he could not have described it this way. He felt like crying. He felt like smashing up something. He felt like, like… he did not know what, but he had to do something. The green wooden gate of the church was wide open. On an impulse Sunny got up and walked out. No one saw him go. No one ever saw him again.

THE BRIDGE

RANJAN KAUL, mostly known as Sunny disappeared in January 1992 and was miraculously brought back to his house in New Delhi in December of that year, by two *coolies* from the railway station in Jullundur. He was twenty years old at that time and had Downs Syndrome. His life on the Jullundur railway station forms the first episode. Much of how Sunny spent his life on the station is from conversations his mother, Raj Kumari had with the *coolies* and with Sunny himself, which she then related to me.

When Raj called me with the incredible news that Sunny had indeed come home, I went at once to visit him. Sunny still had the bushy beard and mop of unruly hair which had grown untended during his time away from home. However, his lopsided grin which I knew so well and his habit of tilting his head to one side were still there. I was told that the first thing he had said on entering his house, was to promise that he would never go out of the house again. But Sunny being Sunny, was soon back at his favorite haunts in the Greater Kailash market. Everyone who had known him and missed him were genuinely happy.

Over many weeks of talking to Sunny, Raj and I put together some facts of what had actually happened to him. However, Sunny kept changing his stories and it was obvious that he had forgotten whatever he told us when he first came back. It is a fact though that when he went away, Sunny could not pronounce the letter 'R'. Necessity had made him learn it. He could now say his name, Ranjan. He also occasionally said things like, "Thanks be to God," inspiring the events with Rev. Paul.

After a period of about three years, in 1995, during which he refused to go back to school but spent his time back on the terrace and in the market, Sunny disappeared again. This time we found him in Calcutta but have no idea whatsoever how he came to be there.

In early 1996, Mr. Kaul called me one day to say he had received news that Sunny was in Calcutta. He had received a letter from a certain gentleman who had sent him details of Sunny and that he was living with him. After his return from Jullundur, Raj and I had talked about how to safeguard our children from the kind of experience Sunny had gone through. Raj had taken the precaution to put a chain round Sunny's neck with his name, address and telephone number on the pendant. However, there was no trace of it when he returned nor did he know what had happened to it. It was made of silver and we could only surmise that somewhere, someone had just pulled it off him. It was because of this that the station master at the station in Jullundur had been unable to help earlier. So, we had done what we thought was a better way of ensuring that if Sunny should wander off again there would be a sure way of identification. Raj got his name and address tattooed on his right forearm. It helped Deepak to contact Sunny's father. We do not know how he got to Calcutta. We think his old 'friends' contacted him once again.

I was attending a conference in Calcutta about the time the letter arrived and I readily agreed to Mr. Kaul's suggestion that I visit the gentleman who had written the letter, and see if the boy he talked about was really Sunny. I did visit as soon as I could and met the family. They knew exactly where Sunny would be at this time of the evening. It was 5.00 p.m. and Sunny was in the fish market. They fetched him for me and he recognized me and smiled in greeting. He looked well. Clean, hair cut, nails pared and happy. I was touched and humbled at how this poor fisherman's family had taken the time to look after Sunny and had made the effort to trace his parents. They were genuinely fond of Sunny, I could see. The second episode is therefore based on what I learnt from Deepak. They did not know how Sunny came to Calcutta. Nor did Sunny. So this will ever remain a mystery. Raj Kumari, in the meantime was diagnosed with cancer. She died before Sunny could be located again.

I write this not to frighten families with children who are intellectually disabled but to warn them of the dangers they may face if adequate precautions are not taken for their safety. I also make a plea to take more seriously the importance of teaching our children to be wary of strangers who befriend them. At the least they should be encouraged to talk of their activities during the day. Today Sunny is 37 years old. He has no memories of his two escapades. His brother and his wife and their charming little ten year old are now Sunny's family and he is fortunate to have them to care for him. But Sunny should be in a facility that could either train him or employ him even on a very nominal income. He has access to neither. Sunny's situation reflects the plight of many like him who languish for want of a supportive infrastructure in our country. Many acts and many conferences and many governmental policies later we still have many Sunny's who have nowhere to go and nothing to do.

This effort is therefore fiction based on what we think happened to Sunny. What happened to Sunny should not happen to any person. Normal or Disabled.

EPISODE THREE: CALCUTTA

CHAPTER I

Dawn. A pearly gray drizzle soaked the docks of Kidderpore in Calcutta with a gentle persistence. It had been raining almost continuously from the previous night but it was not yet the monsoon. The big rains were still a couple of days away. Used to being flooded out year after year, the residents of Kidderpore went about their work with an indifference born out of long tolerance. In the dock area itself, fishing boats had set out as usual and those who waited on shore for their return did so according to their individual characteristics.

The small group around Binoy was engrossed in a game of cards. The wooden shack was filled with acrid smoke from their *beedis* and the sour smell of unwashed sweating bodies. In another part of the docks, Deepak and his brother Kamalu tried to make themselves as comfortable as they could on a pile of gunny sacks. They welcomed this chance to catch up on sleep. Twelve people in a small ten by ten room, which was their home, made it impossible to ever get a full night's sleep. Dreadful were the nights when their father would lurch into the room, drunk on cheap liquor and make signs to his wife and companion of twenty years, Parvathi, to come out on to the small cramped balcony. Parvathi's attempts to keep everything quiet were more pathetic than the sounds, which were clearly audible not only to the family inside the room, but to the neighbors as well.

But all was quiet this gray morning on the docks and sleep seemed a welcome possibility. The peculiar odor of wet wood, gunny sacking and ropes mingled with the all-pervasive smell of fish was soothing because it was familiar. But this peaceful quietness was not destined to remain for long. There was a sudden eruption of noise made by the jarring diesel of a truck, which groaned and screeched to a halt at one of the buildings. It was unusual for a truck to come on to the docks and it brought everyone out. They saw the small bent figure of a boy who stepped out hesitantly with a cloth bundle clutched tightly in his hands and pressed against his chest. Before anyone could comment or start a conversation with the driver of the truck, he revved his engine with an ear-splitting roar and took off at great speed onto the road, which led into the town. This was surprising. Normally truck drivers were a garrulous lot. Ranjan, mostly known as Sunny, for that was his nickname, stood on the dock looking warily at the small group of men who surrounded him. There was a disarming childlike vulnerability about him. To Binoy's group it was an invitation for some entertainment and they were eager to talk. Anything to help them while away the time waiting for the fishing boats to return with the day's catch. Sunny stood silently getting wet in the rain but making no move to gain the shelter of the shacks nearby. When one of the men good naturedly pushed him into the small wooden shed used for storing cane baskets and gunny sacks, he went along docilely and wiped his wet head with the bundle he carried. Without being invited to do so, he made himself comfortable on the pile of sacks just vacated by Deepak. But he still looked frightened. A tremulous lower lip matched the fear and apprehension in his eyes and became more obvious as the men crowded around him with their bantering conversation.

He was not the usual visitor one expected to see in the dock area. He was obviously not one of the henchmen of Tapan, the uncrowned king of Kidderpore. Tapan, it was said had more clout than the politicians who ruled the destinies of Calcutta. "Ask Tapan" or "Tell Tapan" was the standard answer given to anyone who wanted something done. Anything done, in fact. Tapan was always ready to help. For a price, of course. Everything was possible for Tapan. But this boy was not the type. The unkempt mop of hair and a beard made it obvious that he had not seen water or soap for quite some time. No, he was not Tapan's type of man. But then who could tell what Tapan would do? It was best to be polite and tread with care. Even with this unseemly candidate.

Binoy who had ambitions of his own to dethrone Tapan, was more than curious. If this sorry figure was really Tapan's, then Tapan was losing his touch. Binoy felt good at this thought and became authoritative. He led the questioning. "Where did he come from?" they wanted to know. "Who was he? Why had he come here?" Many questions later, they still did not know much about him.

"My name is Sunny," he said over and over again, articulating it carefully, for he seemed to have some difficulty in speaking. "I came here in a truck." He said this with pride and a happy smile lighting up his face momentarily, the fear forgotten. It was as if the ride in the truck in itself was an achievement of some sort and to be cherished. It seemed that Sunny either did not know or was deliberately acting stupid. In answer to their questions he said things which made no sense. Binoy and the two men with him soon grew tired of the newcomer. One thing they were sure of was that Sunny was definitely not Tapan's man. He was a joke. They went back to their game of cards but not before they had made several lewd suggestions to Deepak, who had stood by silently all this while.

Binoy was the undisputed leader of the dockside workers forcing respect and fear in equal measure. But Deepak was known to have helped out many an out of work laborer and by no means the leader that Binoy was. But many would have happily served him had he decided to take on Binoy. Now for Sunny, a benign fate had decreed that it would be Deepak and not Binoy who would take him under his protection.

When Binoy and his men had left, a bemused Deepak sat looking at this boy. Boy? Man? What and who was he? He looked like one of those *Agori sadhus*. Something about him worried Deepak though. He sat quietly enough but with a trusting innocence, which reminded Deepak of his little sister. He had the same quick smile and the desperate eagerness to please was obvious in his manner. Yet he could hardly make himself understood, though if you listened very carefully you could just about make out more or less

117

what he was trying to say. But he was not saying much anyway. Just sitting there as if he belonged here and had been doing it all his life. This was an act of complete trust in strangers, which amazed Deepak and impelled a reluctant sympathy. He was to learn later that it was this peculiar ability that had seen Sunny through many situations, which may have defeated others.

CHAPTER II

It was more than two hours later that the boats came back. However many times one went out to sea, it was always an event when the fishermen came home safe and the boats were safely tied to the strong iron posts hammered onto the wooden planks of the docks. Deepak's other brother, Kanhai, had gone out to day. Kanhai had yet to be broken in and needed many years of experience before he could match the others. He had first begged and then insisted on being allowed to go out on his own. The sense of relief, which the brothers shared on his safe return, made them break out into loud laughter. There was a legend, which every man who went out to sea knew. They had heard it as little children from the other men in the family. Women were not supposed to relate this story for the sea was like a jealous mistress but it could be tolerant and even helpful if the men came out in their boats every day forsaking wives and sweethearts. But if any man preferred to spend more time with his woman when he should have been on the sea it could be aroused to fury. It was also said that if it liked the looks of one of the young men it would quickly and surely take him to her depths to remain there for her pleasure. This was specially so with the new ones and this was but Kanhai's first trip out into the sea. So, even though the catch was small, Deepak was relieved and happy.

Amidst all the shouting and excitement of unloading the catch, everyone had forgotten about Sunny. But the sudden excitement of the boats coming in one by one, the men running up to catch hold of the thick ropes to pull it ashore, the splashing into the sea up to their waists, naked torsos glinting in the pale watery sunlight and the babble of noise brought Sunny out as well. This was a sight Sunny had never seen before and an invitation he could not resist. A wide smile lit up his face. Throwing his bundle on to the floor, he ran up to Deepak's boat and pitched in with happy enthusiasm. He shouted out in agreement to the orders Deepak was giving to the others.

Deepak was directing his brother. "Gently, gently" he said when the boat rocked violently at a sudden swell.

"Gently, gently" echoed Sunny head nodding in approval and a smile of delight on his face.

"Bring it a little to the left, now right. Keep her steady" said Deepak.

"Yes. Yes" said Sunny. Then he echoed Deepak's last sentence. "Keep her steady."

Sunny's sudden joining in as a part of the team so wholeheartedly amused those who had already met him but Kanhai still in the rocking boat, looked at the funny looking man and the way his brothers humored him with a growing sense of premonition. He knew his brother and his invariable succumbing to appeals of all kinds. And guessed very correctly, that he was looking at the latest recipient of Deepak's many acts of kindness. A hot meal perhaps and whatever money could be spared and he would be sent on his way. Kanhai smiled to himself and shook his head ruefully. Deepak and his unfortunate predilection to befriend the many who seemed drawn to him was a family joke.

When the boat was safely tied up to bob gently on the gray green water, the men took the slimy wet net into the wooden shack to decide on what was saleable and what could be discarded or given away to others. Sunny walked back into the shed along with them part of the team now and oblivious to his small bundle of clothes getting tramped upon. It was Deepak who rescued it and handing it to Sunny put his arm around his shoulders.

"Thank you" he said, meaning it genuinely, though the other two laughed, "Thank you for your help." Sunny responded in a spontaneous gesture. Putting his own arms around Deepak, he said.

"It's OK. *Yaar.*"

This, as Deepak and his brothers discovered later, was Sunny's favorite word. *"Yaar"* "Friend." It was unusual and unexpected and they all laughed. But it also made them look at Sunny in a new wondering sort of way.

This acceptance made Sunny's face glow. A shy smile hovered around his lips and he now stood unsure of what he should do or what was expected of him So, he just stood quietly now that the excitement was over, waiting for whatever his new friend would want of him. When the nets were dumped on the ground and opened up he joined the others with eager curiosity, peering first with some apprehension and then with unabashed glee at the sight of the fish still alive and flapping wildly in the net, and thumping their tails on the wooden floor. Sunny laughed excitedly. Scooping up fish in his two hands he allowed them to slither down his arms back into the net. He had never seen anything like this before and this new experience excited him to delirious happiness.

Deepak and his brothers were throwing out the seaweed and the soggy cigarette packets and other wet mementos of the sea, which had come up with the catch. They worked now quickly and in silence and to Kanhai and Kamalu, Sunny's exuberance was becoming irritating. Kanhai told him repeatedly to take his hands out of the net. Sunny obeyed at once but within seconds was back with his hands plunged into the net. Deepak was amused but knew also the reason for his brothers' annoyance. Bruised fish would be so much waste. He did what was the best thing anyone could have done in this situation. With an inborn sense of intuition he took Sunny's hands out of the net gently and showed him that he should take out the fish one by one.

"Gently. Like this" he said, showing him each fish as he took it out of the net and put it into the open wicker baskets on the floor.

Kamalu and Kanhai exchanged glances. "Deepak", the glance said, "What else can you expect from him?" Kanhai nodded his head up and down. When Deepak decided to befriend someone there was no way to stop him. But when Sunny happily picked up globs of sand along with the fish Kanhai could not control himself. Speed was essential. The sooner you got to the market the better the sale would be. But if Deepak wanted to allow this boy to mess up their work he would put a stop to it. He glared at Sunny thinking that would intimidate him. He was rewarded with a huge grin. Enough was enough felt Kanhai. Catching hold of Sunny's hand he gave it a vigorous shake.

"Drop that you idiot," he said, the look in his eyes matching the tone of his voice. It worked like magic.

Immediately subdued, Sunny retreated into a corner of the shed and sat down. His happiness and laughter vanished and he was once again the forlorn frightened person who had got off the truck just an hour ago. Like a little puppy that had been whipped thought Deepak. He looked at Kanhai to reprimand him but saw that Kanhai was still grim faced and angry. Kanhai had not expected such a drastic change in Sunny and this made him feel guilty and in turn more annoyed. A troubled silence descended on all of them and they worked quickly. Kanhai glanced at Sunny every now and then. He was truly aghast. He had not done anything to bring about this picture of abject despair that Sunny now presented. Deepak smiled at Sunny sitting now in the corner, as if to say, "Don't worry." It was not lost on Sunny and he understood its implication an answering smile started slowly and spread into a grateful grin. But he did not venture from his corner again.

Work done the brothers cleaned up the shed for the next catch and prepared to leave. Kanhai and Kamalu looked questioningly at Deepak, the unspoken question of course was "What do we do with this boy?"

Deepak walked out to spread the net out to dry in the sun and his brothers followed him. Sunny too joined them without hesitation, walking along as if it was expected of him. The work done, the trio started to walk out of the docks talking among themselves about their day's responsibilities now. Deepak would sell the fish and both Kanhai and Kamalu would go to the market area where laborers were always in demand to try to get work for the day. Sunny walked behind them but his shoulders drooped because he was unsure whether his new friends wanted him to go along with them to help with the fish or whether he should sit here. They had not specifically told him not to follow them and to Sunny this was an open invitation.

In the short time that he had arrived at the docks he had somehow managed to make Deepak feel as if he was his responsibility. He would have liked to take Sunny back with him rather than leave him on the docks to fend for himself now. But he acknowledged to himself the impossibility of this. He would not be able to take care of this boy who had so suddenly come into his life this morning. So, when they arrived at the end of the docks Deepak stopped. He looked straight into Sunny's eyes. "We are going home," he told Sunny, looking straight into his eyes, so that he understood what he was saying. He did not expect the quick answer. "OK." said Sunny with the whimsical smile lighting up his face once again. "I'll come with you." He nodded his head up and down as if he had no doubt about this. Kanhai snorted with irritation and even Kamalu, the quiet one was forced to say "Impossible. How can he come home with us?"

Deepak looked with concern at Sunny. His brothers were right. There was absolutely no reason for him to stay on and look after Sunny. So he started walking away once again followed by Kamalu and Kanhai until a shout and a laugh made him look back. Kanhai was standing with his hands on his hips pointing to Sunny who was still some distance away but dutifully following them. Kanhai's irritation had gone now that the work had been done and he felt a vague disquiet at the memory of a frightened and cowering Sunny sitting quietly in the corner of their wooden shed on the docks.

Whenever the men stopped, Sunny also stopped. They looked like a still from some movie. Deepak, Kamalu and Kanhai all in a line silhouetted against a gray sky and looking towards the slight figure of Sunny. Whenever this happened apprehension slowly blanched Sunny's face and the trembling lip was back. Deepak sighed hugely. There was only one thing he could do now. Take Sunny home for the time being and then figure out what to do with him. His mind made up he gestured for Sunny to come up and join him. The smile back on his face now, Sunny ran up and stood obediently in front of Deepak looking up at him with a trusting innocence. Just like a little puppy thought Deepak again. Looking back at Kamal and Kanhai, Deepak shrugged his shoulders and gestured for them to follow as well.

Sunny was now transformed into Deepak's helper and friend. "Come On. Come On." he said, copying Deepak's gesture while an unbelieving Kanhai looked on and shook his head in despair. Kamalu, seeing the look on Kanhai's face and Sunny's confident behavior laughed heartily. Sunny did not know why or what the laughter was about but the fact that they laughed told him that he was with people who were happy. So he joined in wholeheartedly making the three brothers look at each with an amusement. Assured now that he was back in favor and keeping step with Deepak, Sunny chattered about the sea and the catch of fish. He talked about the boats and how he would like to go with them into the sea one day. It was as if he had known no other life but this. At any rate, he can make himself useful, thought Deepak glancing at the now ebullient boy walking along beside him.

Careful questioning had not brought out more information than he had already given them unasked. He had come in a truck he said over and over again. It became obvious from his talk that he had been in other places before but names and details were vague and muddled. The one thing, which was certain, was that somewhere at some time he had lived on a station platform and it was he who had helped the station master. Where was this station, Deepak wondered? It was very far away said Sunny. He had to come in a truck. To Sunny it was logical and explained everything. Deepak and his brothers listened with amazement to Sunny's rambling talk, now about a temple and then about trains and about motorcycles and eating his dinner with someone he called Father. The one thing, which became clear as Sunny talked, was that all along, a Divine providence had traveled with him and actually seen to it that he came to no harm. Did this strange boy have some power which forced people to reach down into long dormant depths of their mind and to their own surprise sometimes, go out of their way to help him and do things which they normally would not have done? Sunny himself was happily unaware of the reactions of those who met him. He responded to people as they did to him. It was as simple as that. Now, as far as he was concerned, he had met another man and this man was his brother and his friend. He would give him his unhesitating loyalty because through an inexplicable instinct he could tell that this man was good.

CHAPTER III

Deepak's shop was a small square made of deal wood slats and perched on top of spindly wooden posts. It was one of the many that lined both sides of the street which was known for this. The *Machli walla gully* was the haunt of most of Calcutta, whether one shopped for its famous fish oneself and took home fresh *bhetkis* wrapped in yesterday's newspapers or rolled up to rest lovingly on the cushioned seats of imported cars which brought the *khansamas* of the rich. Fresh fish, straight from the sea into the cooking pot. It had freshness and a flavor for which the native Calcutta-born would give anything. Better than chicken and mutton. Better than anything else in fact. These were the clientele to which Deepak and the others catered. The discerning customer could with one sniff distinguish the evening's catch with the morning's, even a few hours apart. So one had to be careful.

FRESH FISH SOLD HERE.
PROPRIETOR. DEEPAK SHAW.

This proclamation called to the fish eating population of Calcutta. It was a yellow board with red writing on it, nailed slightly crookedly to the top wooden slat of the shop. The board was a contribution from Deepak's sister who had been sent to a school for a couple of years until the fees became too much for the family to bear and the number of children kept increasing steadily each year. Shanta had studied up to the ninth standard and it was a matter of pride to her that she could read the English papers and magazines and share what she read with the rest of her family. Especially Deepak, who was always asking her to read out bits from film magazines he brought home.

Reaching the shop, Deepak told Sunny to sit quietly by his side, which he did with immediate obedience. Some of the others had already started their sale. The shouted out their greeting to Deepak

126

and his brothers. The newcomer with Deepak was not lost on them. They noted the scraggy looking chap but were too busy to give him more than a glance and wonder who he was. Though the catch was not much this day, the sale was good and Deepak and his brother became engrossed with their customers.

Sunny looked on with great interest at first but was not able to sit still for long. Getting down from his place behind Deepak he wandered along the road. He had no particular destination in mind nor did he know where he went. He did know that he was hungry and sleepy. So the thing to do was to find a place to sleep. Just down the road from Deepak's shop Sunny stopped at a large white stucco building. It was big with broad windows, which were firmly shut. White lace curtains could be seen through the window panes. A narrow cemented portion on the front of the house ended in a small wooden gate opening on to the road. Just inside, on the left of the gate was a narrow stairway leading on to the roof. Sunny stood looking in through the gate for some time. It did not occur to him to go in and ask for help. Or ask for food and shelter. He had become accustomed to making the best of whatever he got wherever he was. He looked at the wide space under the staircase. He had slept in such places before. He knew that it would make a comfortable place for him to rest in for some time. It was dry and was sufficient shelter from the thin rain, which persisted. Sunny opened the gate and stooping low to get under the stairway sat down hugging his knees to his chest. The two T-shirts and a pair of shabby jeans which was the bundle he had brought with him and which he had guarded was long forgotten. He did not remember where he had left it. Gradually his head sank on to his knees and soon he was sleeping curled up like a fetus and just as vulnerable.

This is where Kamalu found him after a hectic search. During a lull in the sale of his fish, Deepak had realized that Sunny was no longer sitting behind him. He felt contrite. He should have kept more careful watch. Something about this Sunny made him feel uneasy and he was conscious of a wholly unrealistic impulse to look after him. God knows why, he thought a trifle annoyed. It was none of his business and if he could come from wherever he had come and traveled around in trucks and so on he could surely look after himself. He had obviously done so all these days. But he had come to him, of all the people on the docks. He wished he had never set eyes on him. It did not prevent him however from sending Kamalu, grumbling and reluctant, to find Sunny.

An increasingly irritated Kamalu found Sunny sleeping peacefully under the staircase of a house which belonged to none other than Mr. Chaturlal Bose. Sunny had selected for his siesta the home of a wealthy business tycoon well known in Calcutta. Fortunately there appeared to be no one at home. So, Kamalu did not hesitate in shouting out to Sunny. There was no response. Sunny was fast asleep. Kamalu rattled the gate, getting louder at each shake. There was no response. Kamalu was now really annoyed. He opened the gate and shook Sunny roughly by the shoulder, saying "Get Up. Get up you lazy..." (a Bangla swear word). Sunny was equally determined not to be disturbed and shook off Kamalu's hand, shouting in anger. But Kamalu was the stronger and physically lifted Sunny on to his feet. Sleepy and annoyed Sunny was made to walk back to the *Machli walla gully*. Deepak took out his fear that something had happened to Sunny by shouting at him. "Don't you dare go anywhere without asking me first" he said angrily and wondered at the same time why he had not taken this opportunity to get rid of Sunny once and for all. Sunny was too sleepy to react in any way. He was also angry at being woken up and brought back. So he sulked and stood silently looking down at the ground for some time ignoring Deepak and the others. Finally getting tired of standing, he sat down on the mud in front of Deepak's stall. But he stayed put because he knew that he now belonged to Deepak

It was after eleven in the morning when Deepak wound up business and they were free to go home. He had decided to take Sunny home with him. He would feed this boy who looked starved. Then he would have to figure out what to do with him. When they arrived at their one room home, which they rented in the dock area, his family accepted Sunny unquestioningly. When there were so many people to feed, one more made no difference, said Parvathi, when the boys had come in. It was easier to give when you did not have much to give, but if you had much, giving was a problem. It was a simple and tried truth which Parvathi had known all her life.

During the meal the other children were curious and tried to get Sunny to talk about himself but soon tired of it. It was finally Shanta the educated one in the family, who voiced what they had all felt. This boy was a *budhu*. One of those they had seen often enough in the market place or at *melas*. They were not a danger to anyone really but then they were not much use either. People said that if someone like this Sunny came to your house then you had to be good to them because they were a gift from the gods and sent to them so that they could look after him and thus lessen their bad *karma*. After this discovery everyone looked at Sunny with a little more interest. It was difficult not to like him or to resist that winsome smile.

If his family had so unquestioningly accepted Sunny, thought Deepak, he would really and truly become his responsibility. The question now was what to do with this sudden manifestation of God's mercy. He decided to take him back to his new found shelter under the stairway and let the morning bring some solution to the sudden problem fate had thrust on him. After their meal of rice and a curry made with left over fish heads, Deepak had taken Sunny back to the big white house, which Sunny had chosen, for his temporary abode. The choice of this particular house was not lost on Deepak. He knew like everyone in the locality, that the house belonged to a Mr. Bose who was hardly ever at home. At this time he was away traveling in Europe and the servants who came to clean up every morning came at their own time. It was an amazing coincidence that Sunny had found what seemed to be the perfect place for him to stay. Another indication that some divine being went along with Sunny wherever he went and whatever he did.

For Sunny it made no difference. He had a place to sleep and his stomach was full of rice and fish curry. He could not have been happier. No awkward questions popped into his head wondering why

129

Deepak had brought him back to the staircase. Could he not have slept with the rest of them safe from the rain?

"So, Sunny," said Deepak feeling embarrassed even though he knew that Sunny did not hold him responsible for his having to sleep out in the open. "You sleep here tonight and I will come and take you back to the house in the morning. OK?"

"OK." said a sleepy Sunny. All he wanted to do now was sleep. Now why did I say I will come for him in the morning thought Deepak to himself? It was a good chance to get rid of the boy. He knew that Sunny would not find his way to his house. Even as these thoughts went through his mind, Deepak knew that he would come back in the morning. He would come, if only to satisfy himself that nothing had happened to Sunny during the night.

Sunny, deeply asleep in a matter of minutes knew little of the turmoil he had caused in Deepak's mind.

CHAPTER IV

Deepak could not sleep. Visions of Sunny being chased away from his little niche under the stairs by an angry *chowkidar*, of police dragging a frightened and crying Sunny away to the police station, kept him tossing and turning almost the whole night. Even the long suffering Kamalu, who slept next to him was forced to dig him in the ribs and angrily whisper, telling him to go check on Sunny if he was that worried. This was what Deepak did. He had to be out at the docks by 5 o'clock in the morning to get the best catch and going by way of Sunny's temporary abode was not a problem. Even as he decided this he wondered why he was being so protective and half asleep he still grappled with this strange happening. This boy was a nobody who had just dropped into his life. So what was it that made him his guardian? But the fact was that this boy had been thrust into his life by fate and fate was telling him to look after him and what did he do? Left him snoring under a staircase and that too in a house belonging to Mr. Bose. If he were found there by the *chowkidar* it would be tough on Sunny. Although this particular *chowkidar* was known to Deepak it could mean a lot of cajoling and perhaps a favor in the form of fresh fish. He also knew that while Mr. Bose was away, very little work was done in his house and security was most lax. So, though he had not been happy about leaving Sunny behind he was not unduly worried and finally slept.

But it was not yet 4.00 a.m. when he woke up with a start. His first thought was of Sunny and he sat up, the night's rationalization all gone now. Once again he was berating himself for having been so uncaring and thoughtless. Stepping softly over the sleeping bodies of his brothers and the sleeping forms of his mother and little sister huddled together near the door, he let himself out into the sultry early morning sounds of Calcutta. It was still dark and hazy but Deepak knew where to look and what he saw was a nightmare. Sunny's few belongings lay in stark evidence that Sunny himself was not there. In a panic now, Deepak crawled under the staircase with irrational thoughts flitting through his mind. Perhaps he was really there and he could not see him in the dark. Perhaps someone found him and took him to a better place. But even as the thoughts came up he dismissed them knowing how silly he was being. No. Sunny was definitely not there anymore.

Most people would have been relieved that a potential problem had been taken off their hands. But not Deepak. He was contrite and blamed himself. His rational mind told him that he did not have to be responsible for a wholly fortuitous situation not of his doing at all. This did not help because his emotional mind sent him into a state close to panic. He ran around to the back of the house to peer through the kitchen window. If the *chowkidar* was there that is where he would be. Snoring on the kitchen floor. But there was no one there this morning. The *chowkidar* was absconding or just too drunk and sleeping it off somewhere. Deepak sighed in frustration. How much easier if he had made the boy sleep in his house. He cursed himself, he cursed the *chowkidar* and most of all he cursed Sunny for not being where he should have been. He spat on the ground. Both unusual for Deepak. He went back to the front of the house, looked again under the staircase and in a wholly absurd frame of mind crawled under the staircase to wait for Sunny. He sat there much like Sunny had done, the previous evening, hugging his knees close to his chest. Within half an hour he got his answer. It was not Sunny returning but the *chowkidar*, freshly shaved, bathed and dressed in his khaki uniform. The sight was enough to galvanize Deepak into action and he heaved himself off the floor and crawled out from under the staircase. It was as if a tightly wound coil of apprehensions had suddenly become uncoiled and as relief flooded him he ran forward and held out his hand in greeting. Completely taken aback at the spectacle of Deepak crawling out from under the staircase and the sudden show of camaraderie, the *chowkidar* stopped dead in his tracks. He allowed Deepak to shake his limp hand with a quizzical frown on his face but soon relaxed to smile hugely at him showing pan stained teeth. This was Deepak. He liked Deepak and was ready to help. He obviously needed something from him but what? Of course he would help particularly if it meant fresh *bhetki*. He could imagine the gut wrenching, mouthwatering aroma of *bhetki* sizzling in mustard oil. Sooo…Sooo… thoughts whizzed around his head. Here was Deepak crawling out from under the staircase. What had happened? *Acha.* Perhaps he was thrown out of his house? Unlikely. May be a late night rendezvous with a girlfriend. No way. Perhaps drunk? Even more unlikely. *Nahi nahi.* Deepak had the reputation of a loner and a very straight guy. One did not associate Deepak with liquor or even girls, strange though it seemed. Very rarely did he even shake anyone's hand let alone grin at them like he did just now. Why he had almost hugged him. But the bizarre behavior was soon explained.

"Sunny?" said a baffled *chowkidar*. A strange looking boy? Of course he had not been doing his *chowkidar* last night but Deepak need not know that he decided prudently.

"Well" said the *chowkidar*, when he had heard Deepak out. "You can see there is no one there now," he said hoping that this Sunny person was not hiding somewhere. This would put him into major trouble. Bose *Babu* was not an easy man to please. What Deepak had said made sense. A sudden guest and no place to sleep. So under Bose *Babu's* staircase was the obvious choice.

"Why not?" he reasoned to himself specially if it was Deepak's friend. But aloud he only said "I will keep an eye out for him. Don't worry. He will be back I am sure. I will let you know." He nodded his head reassuringly and walked off, indicating that he was a busy man with things to do. Deepak watched him go with a strange churning of emotions: fright, sadness, and frustration. A miserable refrain kept popping up in his head pointing a finger and saying "if only". What had happened to Sunny and why was he acting as if his own brother had been lost.

As Deepak walked away, head sunk and a frown on his face, he heard a shout behind him.

"Arre Deepak." said the *chowkidar.* "You know, that *bhetki* you gave me last time. It was delicious. I just wanted to thank you again. Wife enjoyed it. You know what I mean." He laughed loudly at his wit and the implications of his statement.

Deepak nodded his head. He understood. If the *chowkidar* gave him news of Sunny it would be for the price of one fresh *bhetki* fish. But only if there was news. Otherwise it was a no deal. Both knew the rules and both nodded in agreement. The arrival or not of the *bhetki* would depend on Sunny. How weird. How utterly unimaginable that the *chowkidar*'s fish dinner tonight was in Sunny's hands! Deepak had to laugh in spite of the misery which clutched his heart like claws.

CHAPTER V

Mr. Chaturlal Bose was no ordinary man. Born into a family of scholars he was considered a no good, an eccentric. Soon all reservations about how his life would turn out vanished to be replaced by a grudging admiration when he astounded everyone by establishing himself at the very heart of Kolkata's business community. When he opted for a career in business rather than the respected profession of his four elder brothers and his father and grandfather before him, there were many who shook their heads and said "Not him. Not our Chaturlal. He has no head for business." All his brothers were professors in various colleges around the city of Calcutta. One was even abroad and head of a very prestigious business college. In his family, he was the epitome of success and was highly reputed even as his earning a huge salary in dollars was talked about at family gatherings in reverential whispers.

But the excitement of jumping headlong into untested business waters was what kept Chaturlal Bose alive. It was a dangerous game that he played and he often thought of himself as a lion, hidden among the green undergrowth of the jungle and watching the rest of the animals go about their business of existing for that day. The intellectual stimulation that preceded his pounce upon an unsuspecting animal pumped enough adrenalin to keep him going for a long time. It was always small businesses. Businesses in trouble, sinking, sick, the charismatic leader dead and no one to replace him. He was able to contact, convince and win over these houses of trade and turn them around into modestly functioning and modestly earning institutions. Sometimes he took them over completely until he found someone or some other agency to hand them over to at a price and sometimes he charged a fee. He did these seemingly impossible feats of turning around half dead businesses slinking down into darkness and eventual death into the full glare of a life-giving sun by a combination of intuition, personal charisma and shrewd analytical and business sense which no one had taught him.

No one, least of all members of his family, knew how he came by these gifts and they made no pretext of even understanding him. No one in the family had dabbled in business before and he was a wholly unexplainable phenomenon. The brother living abroad however, often lamented the fact that if only Chaturlal had the sense to come and join him there, his shrewd business skills would soon have people knocking on his door.

But Chaturlal Bose was a name that commanded immediate respect in Calcutta and this is what he valued. Stay home and earn the respect and admiration of his fellow beings. This was his philosophy, and if not many shared his view of the world, no one would have faulted him for being tight fisted. In fact the stories about his many good works were the stuff of romance and legend. If his personality did not show this then his imposing house certainly did. Imported Italian marble, original paintings, lush carpets and whatever came out in foreign magazines on décor that he fancied was his within months. Perhaps not many would live comfortably in a mishmash of furniture and art from different periods and different styles. But to Chaturlal Bose this was home and he was proud of it.

Chaturlal had completed a successful trip visiting many of his associates all over Europe. Now back in India and thanks to the vagaries of the airlines he frequented he had to cut short his last meeting and come home much earlier than planned. Chaturlal was always delighted at unexpected twists in his path through life and when he came home in the early hours of the morning to find the house locked, no *chowkidar* in sight and a ragamuffin who looked abnormal sleeping under the stairs that led to his terrace, his mind began analyzing this situation trying to arrive at a reasonable answer to the sight before him. His car was parked as always under the portico but the *sardar* driver he employed had not been told he was arriving that day. But the *chowkidar* should have been there guarding his house. Obviously he was not there and had no inkling that a stranger was actually sleeping under the staircase of the house he was supposedly guarding! Of course he did not expect him back two days early. Chaturlal realized he did not know enough about the man he had employed to guard his house! He made a mental note to rectify the situation immediately. He was annoyed with himself. He looked around at the silent sleeping houses on his street. The only way to get some answers was to wake up this boy and ask him some questions. He shook the boy awake vigorously taking, holding him by his shoulders and taking out his annoyance on the sleeping boy. Sunny sat up, wide eyed and staring. What was happening now? He shook off the restraining hands on his shoulders with a fierce shake of his shoulders and a half sobbing shout as if to say leave me alone. Of all the things he hated most, it was being woken up when he did not want to wake up. He did not like being shaken like that. He did not like being woken up. He shook himself free. He knew from having been in such situations before that most probably what would happen now was that he would be asked to get up and leave. He had experience of facing such men as this one before him now. They always told him what to do and where to go. This had happened many times before. When he was told to go, sometimes angrily, sometimes with shouts and sometimes cajolingly as if he was a child, it always ended in his having to look for a new place. He had no idea why but this is what always happened to him. He did not even begin to wonder who this man was or why he was being woken up. So, he slowly crawled out from under the staircase without a word and began walking away, all without a word.

Chaturlal had not said a word to him and was expecting to get some answers from this boy. Chaturlal was quite taken aback. As Sunny walked past him, his clothes forgotten under the staircase, Chaturlal put out his hand to stop him. Sunny ducked and lowered his head, thinking that he was going to be beaten and stood passively waiting for the blow to fall. Chaturlal, for once in his life was nonplussed. What a strange reaction. How sad. For some reason he felt a queasy feeling in his stomach, a sort of remorse, as if he had actually beaten a small defenseless child. He felt he should apologize to this boy for waking him up! He had done nothing and said nothing and yet this boy had ducked as if he was going to thrash him. He did look frightened now. Why did he think he was going to beat him?

Only the silent poles with fluorescent night lights were witness to this strange happening under the staircase of Chaturlal Bose's house.

In the light from the street lamps now Chaturlal looked closely at the boy standing solemnly as if awaiting a verdict. Guilt was not an emotion that Chaturlal knew or confronted often. But the sight of this boy evoked long forgotten memories of school and a boy who looked like this one did. *'Anadi'* they called him affectionately for that was what he was. *'Anadi'* or 'Innocent'.

The most innocent and the most gullible person he and his friends had ever met. Yet with such charm and a sort of a smiling appeal that they all went out of their way to hear him out and help him whenever required. But he had become fiercely loyal to Chaturlal. Yes. This boy was like his friend Anadi. Sunny's look of absolute incomprehension tinged with a wariness brought Chaturlal Bose to his senses. What was he doing trying to talk to this boy who was half asleep anyway?? It was asinine of him. Ridiculous. Now that he had taken a close look at him he knew that this boy was what they called Downs Syndrome, like his friend and *chela* of long ago and long forgotten. He had been in the same class for several years and was still there when Chaturlal had finished his schooling. He had discovered that all it took to get work out of him was one kind word. Soon he had *Anadi* carry his school bag, polish his shoes if dirty and do many odd jobs which he did with dogged faithfulness which gradually became such an embarrassment to Chaturlal that he would have done anything to stop *Anadi* following him around. But it was too late, and all *Anadi* had wanted was to serve him. Chaturlal remembered the initial amusement, the ribbing from his friends and classmates and then the gradual feeling of guilt which had replaced all other emotions. But that was a long time ago.

Going closer to the bay now he put his hand on his arm to show him that he meant no harm. "A*rre, Arre*" he said in Bengali now to Sunny. "Don't be frightened. I just wanted to ask you if you saw the *chowkidar.*" All he got was an uncomprehending stare. Chaturlal tried again, this time in Hindi. Sunny stood silently staring at the man and there was an air of expectancy about him. All he was concerned about was that he would go if he was asked to go. He would sleep again if he was allowed to do so. It was as simple as that. Getting nowhere with him Chaturlal decided to leave him to sleep under the staircase and perhaps if he was still there when he came back in the morning he would decide what to do with him. As for him, he would spend the rest of the night in his sister's house, which fortunately was not too far away and on the same street.

Chaturlal thanked his lucky stars that his sister lived close by and that a welcoming bed and food would be provided. Then he had the task of dealing with his errant *chowkidar*. The wretched man was most probably drunk. So, he walked back to the taxi which had been waiting patiently. On the point of getting in he turned around to see the boy still standing where he had left him and still looking at him. A relieved Sunny realized that he could now go back to sleep in his chosen haven under the stairs. The man had not shouted and had not told him to go away from there. He should be nice to this nice man although he had woken him up. So, he lifted his hand and waved to Chaturlal. It looked as if he was saying "Thank you for your visit" to a friend who had dropped by. Chaturlal totally surprised laughed out aloud. Sunny's gesture changed the whole course of events for both of them. It was 2.00.a.m.

Chaturlal Bose, did not know this, but he was about to become yet another benefactor of Sunny and on his way to becoming an integral thread in the web of support that was amazingly and mysteriously being spun around him lest he fall and hurt himself. Chaturlal waved back at Sunny and then in a moment of madness he could not explain shouted out to him to come with him and get into the taxi. Responding to the authority in the man's voice, Sunny asked no questions. He walked over and got into the front seat and waited. The taxi took him and Chaturlal to his sister's house, who though woken up in the middle of the night was delighted to see her brother, particularly since he never visited her much. She fussed around him and although she noticed the funny looking boy he had brought with him she was ready to give him a bed and got both of them hot, highly sugared tea. Sunny was given a pillow and a *dhari* to spread over the carpet in the drawing room and asked to sleep there till the morning. From long practice in adjusting to new situations often not of his making, Sunny lost no time in making himself at home. He was happy and content. He liked sugared tea, he liked the brightly colored *dhari*, which was his bed and he liked the man who had been kind to him. He asked for nothing more.

By six o'clock that morning, just when Deepak had left the *chowkidar*, everyone in the vicinity knew that the big boss Chaturlal Bose had returned from his foreign tour. The driver of the truck bringing in vegetables to the market had seen Chaturlal passing by in his taxi and he told the milk man who told the women coming for domestic work in the houses in the area and they alerted Munni who worked in Chaturlal's house. He was not due till tomorrow but if he had returned Munni knew that her job was to go and clean and prepare the house for him. She hurried over to the house and met the *chowkidar* who was making himself comfortable in the portico and watched gleefully as he digested this news and its implications.

Chaturlal, like Deepak, did not sleep at all. He got up to read. After some time though his thoughts turned to the boy sleeping the sleep of the innocent in his sister's drawing room. Who was he and how and why had he ended up sleeping under the staircase in his house? He got up from his bed and stepped softly into the drawing room and looked down at the sleeping Sunny. There was something he could not quite define stirring in his heart. He remembered long forgotten emotions and situations with *Anadi*. Many of these memories made him smile with sad fondness for the boy who had been so devoted to him and whom he had left behind without even a single thought. He wondered now what had happened to *Anadi*.

Sunny stirred in his sleep and sighed and threw his arm over his head. It was a sad sound and lonely. It was then that Chaturlal saw the tattoo on his forearm. Curious, he bent down to take a closer look and not being able to read in the darkness of the room he switched on the light hoping it would not wake the boy up. It did not. Sunny slept on, as soundly as before and looked as if he was used to sleeping on the floor like this all his life. Chaturlal shook his head in amazement when he read the inscription on the boys arm. It clearly stated that his name was Ranjan Kaul. Underneath in smaller letters was his address.

CHAPTER VI

It did not take Chaturlal any time at all to call the number tattooed on the boys arm. Briskly business-like now he told the gentleman who picked up the phone on the other end about finding Sunny. He was embarrassed at the torrent of gratitude which poured out of the telephone. After all, all he had done was come home in the middle of the night. Even as he said that, he realized that had he not done so, he would never have discovered the sleeping boy and his life would not have taken the course it now did.

The next morning, Sunny sat obediently in the drawing room. Having washed and eaten a good breakfast he was now ready to do the bidding of his new friend. The two children of the house stood in the doorway and looked curiously at this strange looking person. The servants poked their heads in occasionally to take a look at the boy who had been brought in late in the night by their own Chaturlal *Babu*. They had heard stories about him but never had he brought home someone so weird like this boy, who just sat there and stared at them as if they were the odd looking ones and not him.

Sunny did not mind being left alone while Chaturlal arranged for train tickets and for someone to take this boy to his home. Several phone calls later to Delhi, everything was arranged. He got two tickets for Delhi by that night's sleeper, called the telephone number tattooed on Sunny's arm and gasped in amazement when he heard that this boy, Ranjan Kaul, his name he learnt was Sunny for short, had been missing for one whole year. He could not even begin to imagine such a situation. This meant that Sunny had been absolutely wide open for exploitation and extremely vulnerable for a whole year. Yet here he was, completely hale and hearty, looking as if he had been looked after and cared for and had never felt a twinge of fear or want. What in God's name was he doing with himself, this Sunny, all these months on end. Where had he been? How had he survived? That was the most amazing question of all. Adrift in a world ever ready to swallow the wicked and the innocent alike, Sunny had somehow managed to keep afloat, avoiding the rapids and seemingly sailed along just fine. He had not ended up in the pits involved with drugs and sex, or as part of the sick, the wounded and the rejects of life that each metropolis threw up as its unwanted effluence. Chaturlal came close to believing in a just God who was more faithful to you then you were to Him.

Before going back to his own home, Chaturlal who was being consumed with curiosity, sat down next to Sunny and over many cups of sweet tea tried to prize out his story. What a story that would make he thought, if only he could get this boy to talk. Some of his questions got vague unconnected answers and some went unanswered except for blank stares. He did get fascinating glimpses though, of trains and stations and fish and boats. And people. Names of people. Many names, all tumbling one into another, seemingly disjointed from the situations he talked about such as flagging the trains on and off. This brought a huge smile of sheer glee to Chaturlal.

When it was time for Sunny to board the train he went quietly with Chaturlal's servant who had been deputed to reach him home. "Thank you" he said politely to Chaturlal, then to his sister and even to the two little brats who peeped at him from behind the curtains. Chaturlal and his sister's family watched him go. Chaturlal was conscious of vague feelings, wholly unexplained and illogical as if he had just taken part in some major event. He, whose very words were eagerly waited for by many in Calcutta, was silent and yes, grateful that Sunny had turned to say "Thank you". Sunny sat quietly during the ride to the station but gradually got more and more excited as they neared the station. As the man reported to Chaturlal later, "it looked as if he knew all about trains and had sometime actually been in one." He sat smiling and nodding his head and laughed out aloud at the many sights he saw on the station platform. "It was weird" he said. "I began to think that he had actually lived on the station platform all his life."

Early in the morning at about 7.00 am, exactly one year to the day that Sunny had disappeared, the bell rang in the Kaul residence. Raj who had been up the whole night ran to open the door.

"I am home", said Sunny softly. He tilted his head to one side and smiled a lopsided smile.

THE END

SAMADHAN www.samadhanindia.org, an NGO with dual focus on persons with intellectual disability also impacted by poverty was established in 1981 and now works from two centers in Dakshinpuri and Dwarka in New Delhi. Our philosophy is that all persons with intellectual disability can be helped, if appropriate and timely services are available. Over the years SAMADHAN has effectively transferred this philosophy into action and developed a viable model of service delivery, using locally available resources and materials. SAMADHAN's strategy is to link services for the intellectually disabled with the needs of their mothers and the women in the community.

Glossary of Terms

A

Acha – OK/yes

Agori Sadhu – Hindu holy men who took vows to remain unshaved for specific periods

Amma – mum/mother

Anadi – illiterate (innocent)

Arre – exclamation

Arre. Arre. Arre – Oh! Oh! Oh!

Aloo gobi – potatoes & cauliflower

Aloo paratha – potato bread dish (popular breakfast)

B

Baba – boy, term of endearment

Babu – gentleman

Baraat - groom's wedding procession in North India

Bas. Bas. – stop, enough!

Beedi – rolled tobacco leaf (cigarette)

Bhetki – river fish/barramundi

Beta – son

Bhai / Bhaiya(s) – brother(s)

Bhajans – Hindu religious songs

Bhaji – savory flat cake or ball of vegetables, fried in batter

Bhima – a legendary figure in the Hindu epic Mahabharata, known for his strength and fighting skills

Budhu – foolish

C

Chai – Indian tea made with tea leaves, milk, sugar and spices

Chalo, Chalo, Bachon – come on children

Chappatis – Indian bread

Chela – disciple

Chole Bhature – chickpeas with fried wheat bread

Chowkidar – sentry/security

Chutney – dip, a savory accompaniment
Coolies – porters

D
Dal – thick purée or soup made from lentils
Dhabi – roadside food stalls/cafés
Dhari – cotton carpet
Dosas – pancake like breakfast food
Dost – friend

H
Halwa – sweet dish

J
Jalebi – syrupy sweet

K
Khansamas – cooks
Karma – fate

L
Lallu – fool
Lassi – butter milk, yoghurt drink

M
Machli walla gulley – Fishmongers alleyway
Mali – gardener
Mela – gathering or fair

N
Na Baba – no way!
Nahi Nahi – no, no
Nullah – gutter
Nari Niketan – home for girls

P
Paan - betel leaves prepared and used as a stimulant

Pakoras – fried lentil savory
Puri – fried wheat bread
Puri stall – stall selling fried bread
Puris and Bhaji – fried bread with cooked vegetables
Puri wallah – man selling puris

R
Razai – quilt

S
Saab/Sahib – sir
Sala – a term of abuse, sometimes used affectionately
Sambar – South Indian dish of savory lentil as accompaniment to dosas
Sardar – ethnic group mostly in North India

T
Tiffin – lunch/snack
Toba – abjuring sin; good heavens
Tulsi – plant considered to have healing and spiritual properties

W
Wallah – seller

Y
Yaar – friend (colloquial)

L - #0182 - 010719 - C0 - 210/148/8 - PB - DID2554722